Faithful & Devoted:
To My Adelaide

A Quilted Love Story

by Sarah Maxwell
and Dolores Smith

Dedication

By **sharing** the story of Addie and Charles, I hope to remind everyone of the power of love as we are taught in *1 Corinthians 13:1-13:*

> Love is patient, love is kind. It does not envy, it does not boast, it is not proud. It is not rude it is not self-seeking, it is not easily angered, it keeps no record of wrongs. Love does not delight in evil but rejoices with the truth. It always protects, always trusts, always hopes, always perseveres. Love never fails.

This book is dedicated to my amazing husband, Joe, who unfailingly shows his love for me, our family, and his fellow man every day. Thanks, Joe, for all you do.

With my love, Sarah

To Brian, my husband of 29 years. He has been my life though the laughs and the tears and has supported me in my ventures with little complaining.

Thank you for our two wonderful boys. I know our life has been trying since the loss of our son Ryan and his girlfriend, Breigha. Thank you for the way you have helped our son, Kyle, on his way to adulthood. I see a lot of you in him and for that I am grateful. I know Kyle's life with Dharti will be a good one, because he has learned so much from you.

So, I consider myself to be lucky to have been in the right place on July 5, 1981.

- Dolores

Faithful & Devoted: To My Adelaide
A Quilted Love Story

By Sarah Maxwell and Dolores Smith

Editor: Jenifer Dick
Technical Editor: Nan Doljac
Book Design: Kelly Ludwig
Photography: Aaron T. Leimkuehler
Illustration: Lon Eric Craven
Production assistance: Jo Ann Groves

Published by
Kansas City Star Books
1729 Grand Blvd.
Kansas City, Missouri, USA 64108

First edition, first printing
ISBN: 978-1-935362-93-7
Library of Congress Control Number: 2011933526

Printed in the United States of America by Walsworth Publishing Co., Marceline, MO
To order copies, call StarInfo at (816) 234-4636 and say "Books."

PickleDish.com
The Quilter's Home Page

Contents

Introduction **5**

Making the Quilts

   Adelaide **6**

   Charlie **8**

Faithful and Devoted

Chapter 1 .... **10**

   Block 1: All Hallows

Chapter 2 .... **14**

   Block 2: Summer Wind

Chapter 3 .... **17**

   Block 3: Sawtooth

Chapter 4 .... **20**

   Block 4: Wyoming Valley

Chapter 5 .... **24**

   Block 5: Five Spot

Chapter 6 .... **28**

   Block 6: Auntie's Chain

Chapter 7 .... **34**

   Block 7: Kansas Star

Chapter 8 .... **37**

   Block 8: Windmill

Chapter 9 .... **41**

   Block 9: Crown of Thorns

Chapter 10 .... **45**

   Block 10: Salute to the Colors

Chapter 11 .... **49**

   Block 11: Wild Goose Chase

Chapter 12 .... **53**

   Block 12: Cross and Square

Embroidery Instructions for Charlie **57**

Pieced Setting for Adelaide Blocks **66**

Pieced Setting for Charlie Blocks **68**

Finishing for Adelaide Quilt **70**

Finishing for Charlie Quilt **72**

More Quilts

   Rocky Mountain Stars **74**

   Crossing Paths **82**

   Blue Ridge Baskets **86**

   Autumn Ties **90**

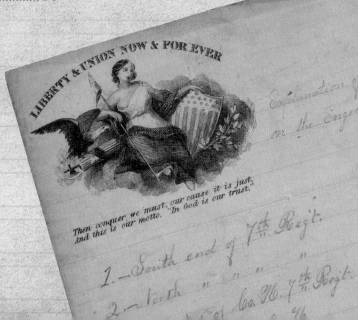

About The Authors

In 2002, Dolores Smith and Sarah Maxwell opened their quilt shop, Homestead Hearth, located in Mexico, Mo. Under that trade name they have since designed quilts that have appeared in most of the major quilting magazines. Their original pattern line debuted in 2009, and is available at their website, www.homesteadhearth.com. They also design fabric for Marcus Fabrics.

Dolores lives in Mexico with her husband. She has two sons. Sarah also lives in Mexico with her husband and two daughters.

Dolores Smith, left, and Sarah Maxwell are the owners of Homestead Hearth in Mexico, Missouri.

Acknowledgements

Writing and publishing a book requires the help and support of so many people beyond the authors. We want to specifically thank the following people:

Faye Burgos for the beautiful fabric that made this project come alive. If Adelaide and Charlie were around they would approve of how Faye translated their love story onto fabric. Keep up the good work!

The team at Marcus Brothers: Stephanie, Pati , Regina and Indra. This group of ladies has been a source of support and inspiration to us for several years now. Thanks for believing in us and helping us achieve some of our dreams.

All of our girls at the shop – Dawn, Lori, Sue, Jane, Deanna, Taylor, Carol, Delana and Allison. They keep us from pulling out all of our hair and keep us smiling. Plus, we can't forget our new mascot, Sir Oliver Winston – he reminds us every day that he is the most important "person" at the shop!

The University of Virginia library for allowing us to share the story of Addie and Charlie and for all their help with our research.

And last, but not least, the crew at Kansas City Star for giving us this opportunity: Diane McLendon and Doug Weaver for seeing the potential in Addie and Charlie's letters; Jenifer Dick for her patience and wonderful suggestions that will make this our best book to date; Aaron Leimkuehler for showcasing the quilts with his excellent photography; Kelly Ludwig for the beautiful design; and to Nan Doljac, technical editor; Eric Craven, illustrator; and Jo Ann Groves, production assistance.

Charles Tenney, center

Adelaide Case

Introduction

I**n 1861,** a young man, Charles Tenney, began his service as a private in Company H of the Seventh Ohio Regiment as Ohio joined other states fighting to preserve the Union. Just before he began service, Tenney traveled to the Mecca, Ohio home of his commander, Hal Case, where he met Hal's sister, Adelaide. As Tenney travels across the county and experiences combat, he details his daily life in a series of letters to Adelaide. She responds to Charlie's letters and their friendship grows. As the war progresses, Charles reveals his affection for Adelaide and their love story develops.

THE WAR AROUND THEM

As tensions between northern and southern states erupted into war in April 1861, thousands of men answered the call to fight for their state. During the four years of the war, approximately 4,000,000 men left home to fight for their beliefs. Many of these soldiers were young with the average age being only 25. Far from home, often suffering brutal conditions, many soldiers turned to letter-writing as a way to stay in touch with those back home.

THE LETTERS

In May 2000, Corinne Carr Nettleton donated an amazing collection to the University of Virginia Library. The collection included about 150 items, including photographs and letters between Adelaide Case and Charles Tenney. The letters provide a detailed look into the life of a soldier and the hardships and worries of those left at home. Charles had a gift for writing and was able to bring the day-to-day life of a soldier to life through his stories. Adelaide was a bit more proper and her letters reveal the strict moral code she felt bound by and her internal battles over whether it was proper to love Charlie.

A NOTE ABOUT THE LETTERS

For clarity and ease of understanding, we have made minor changes in the grammar and punctuation of the letters presented herein. Grammatical errors in the original letters that do not cause confusion remain. At times, the condition of the letters made it impossible to determine some of the text in which case the reader will see a [?].

Adelaide

Adelaide

SIZE: 93 1/2" X 119"
BLOCKS: 6" FINISHED WITH PIECED SETTING MAKING THE BLOCKS 25 1/2" FINISHED
MADE BY DOLORES SMITH AND SARAH MAXWELL
QUILTED BY CONNIE GRESHAM

Fabric Requirements

Adelaide was made using the fabric line, Adelaide by Marcus Fabrics. If you would like to make your quilt in the same fabrics, use the Marcus Fabrics numbers (SKUs) found in parenthesis on the list below. A flyer showing swatches of the fabrics is found on page 94. If you choose to use your own fabrics, substitute with fabrics similar to the swatches.

For the 6" blocks

A variety of creams (1 1/8 yards total):
* 3/8 yard of Cream 1 (2764-0111)
* 1/4 yard of Cream 2 (2774-0142)
* 1/4 yard of Cream 3 (2775-0142)
* 1/4 yard of Cream 4 (2767-0113)

A variety of reds (1 1/4 yards total):
* 1/3 yard of Red 1 (2768-0111)
* 1/4 yard of Red 2 (2771-0111)
* 1/4 yard of Red 3 (2775-0111)
* 1/4 yard of Red 4 (2770-0111)
* 1/8 yard of Red 5 (2769-0111)

A variety of greens (1 1/3 yard total):
* 1/3 yard of Green 1 (2770-0116)
* 1/4 yard of Green 2 (2772-0116)
* 1/4 yard of Green 3 (2768-0116)
* 1/4 yard of Green 4 (2771-0116)
* 1/4 yard of Green 5 (2769-0116)

A variety of browns (3/8 yard total):
* 1/4 yard of Brown 1 (2770-0113)
* 1/8 yard of Brown 2 (2769-0113)

For the pieced setting surrounding the 6" blocks

* 3 3/4 yard of Cream 1 (2764-0111)
* 2 1/4 yard Red 1 (2768-0111)
* 1 1/2 yard Green 4 (2771-0116)
* 1 1/4 yard Red 4 (2770-0111)
* 1 yard Green 1 (2770-0116)
* 3/4 yard Red 5 (2769-0111)
* 3/4 yard Cream 3 (2775-0142)

For the pieced borders

* 2 1/8 yard Red 6 (2765-0142)
* 1 yard Cream 2 (2774-0142)
* 1 yard of Red 5 (2769-0111)

For the binding

* 1 yard Red 7 (2769-0126)

Making the blocks

Individual instructions for each 6" block begin on page 12. Once the blocks are made, you'll need to add a pieced setting surrounding the block to make it finish at 25 1/2". These instructions are on page 66. Once all the blocks are made, use the finishing instructions on page 70 to complete the quilt.

Charlie

Charlie

SIZE: 93 1/2" X 119"
BLOCKS: 12 – 6" FINISHED WITH PIECED SETTING MAKING THE BLOCKS 18" FINISHED
6 – 18" FINISHED EMBROIDERED SETTING BLOCKS
MADE BY DOLORES SMITH AND SARAH MAXWELL
QUILTED BY CONNIE GRESHAM

Fabric Requirements

Charlie was made using the fabric line, Adelaide by Marcus Fabrics. If you would like to make your quilt in the same fabrics, use the Marcus Fabrics numbers (SKUs) found in parenthesis on the list below. A flyer showing swatches of the fabrics is found on page 94. If you choose to use your own fabrics, substitute with fabrics similar to the swatches.

For the 6" blocks

A variety of cream prints (1 3/4 yards total):
* 2/3 yard of Cream 1 (2764-0150)
* 1/3 yard of Cream 2 (2774-0142)
* 1/3 yard of Cream 3 (2775-0142)
* 1/4 yard of Cream 4 (2767-0113)
* 1/4 yard of Cream 5 (2774-0113)
* 1/8 yard of Cream 6 (2771-0142)

A variety of blues (1 2/3 yards total):
* 1/2 yard of Blue 1 (2771-0150)
* 1/4 yard of Blue 2 (2775-0150)
* 1/4 yard of Blue 3 (2772-0150)
* 1/4 yard of Blue 4 (2770-0150)
* 1/4 yard of Blue 5 (2768-0150)
* 1/8 yard of Blue 6 (2773-0150)

A variety of browns (1 yard total):
* 1/3 yard of Brown 1 (2770-0113)
* 1/3 yard of Brown 2 (2769-0113)
* 1/4 yard of Brown 3 (2772-0113)

For the pieced setting surrounding the 6" blocks
* 2 3/4 yards of Cream 6 (2771-0142)
* 2 1/4 yards of Blue 4 (2770-0150)
* 1 yard of dark Brown 1 (2770-0113)

For the embroidery background and sashing
* 1 3/8 yards of aged canvas (WR2-Y139-0141) or muslin
* 1 3/8 yard of Blue 2 (2775-0150)

For the pieced borders
* 2 1/8 yards of Blue 7 (2765-0150)
* 1 yard of Blue 6 (2773-0150)
* 1 yard of Cream 5 (2774-0113)

For the setting triangles
* 2 3/8 yards of Cream 1 (2764-0150)

For the binding
* 1 yard of Blue 8 (2776-0150)

Additional supplies
* Blue embroidery floss to match Blue 2 and needle

Making the blocks

Individual instructions for each 6" block begin on page 13. Once the blocks are made, you'll need to add a pieced setting surrounding the block to make it 18" finished. These instructions are on page 68. These pieced blocks alternate with embroidered blocks. Instructions for those begin on pg 57. Once all the blocks are made, use the finishing instructions on page 72 to complete the quilt.

Faithful and Devoted: to my Adelaide
A Quilted Love Story

When **Charles** Tenney, a young Union soldier, has a chance meeting with the sister of one of his officers, he is instantly captivated. After one meeting, he asks her if he could write to her while he is away. To his delight, she agrees.

With the war raging around them, Charles and Adelaide fall in love through a series of remarkably preserved letters. We read as Charles courts Adelaide while witnessing to her his experiences in battle. And in her letters to Charles, we watch as she recounts her experiences on the home front all while her feelings for him develop from simple friendship to deep and profound love.

Then conquer we must, our cause it is just,
And this is our motto, "In God is our trust."

CHAPTER 1

Addie's **first** preserved letter to Charles is dated January 19, 1861 prior to the start of the war. Already, tension across the United States is rising due to conflict over slavery, worsening economic conditions in the South and political activity which would prevent expansion of slave-holding in new territories and states of the Union. The letter clearly shows that Addie senses danger is near. She begins by addressing Charlie as "my dear brother." She goes on to describe how she hopes their relationship will develop into the closeness shared by siblings. "...I should so love to win your confidence as a sister should her brother's confidence."

Addie acknowledges that Charles is facing difficulty. "...How willingly would I take your position in this war if I could do so, how thankful I ought to be for having brothers and friends to go and protect our homes as I have but when I think of what may come, it causes a trembling fear to take possession of my frame and I sometimes wish that my friends would stay with me."

Addie closes her letter with "Affectionately your sister, ever, Addie." Clearly in early 1861, she viewed herself as a friend to Charles, nothing more.

By June 1861, the couple has exchanged additional letters and on June 16, Charles bravely asks "My dear friend, would you be offended if I were to say My dear Addie? For I'm sure I would much rather call you by the name my heart prompts me to." In six short months, the couple's correspondence has prompted Charles to develop some feelings for Addie beyond the brother-sister relationship she has suggested. He goes on to describe his daily routine at Camp Dennison in Ohio and invites Addie to visit him before his regiment departs for Virginia. Describing his military life-style Charles writes:

"Altogether this is pleasant. There is something fascinating in it to me. I am healthier, stronger and can do more here than in any other business. But there is something more fascinating and that is Addie Case. But I dare not hope that you think more of me than a common friend. If I could only know that you do, how happy I would be. . . .

Meanwhile, I remain, yours truly & affectionately,
Charlie Tenney

P.S. Would you have any objection to our exchanging ambrotypes? If not, I will send mine next time I write."

Addie quickly replies to Charles' request, responding on June 23, 1861:

Dear Friend

After receiving your very welcome letter last evening, I [set] myself to comply with your request to write you. Your letter gave some very pleasant feelings and again some feelings amounting almost to pain because I thought there was a little considerable, of flattery mingled with it. Perhaps if you had been in the room when I read your letter, you might have seen me indulge a very little in that feminine weakness of blushing for indeed I was surprised. There is always some thing so disgusting to flattery in any form and especially when it is from those that I wish to call by the enduring name of friend that for the moment it creates within my heart a strange sensation that is hard to conquer I do not say this as a reproof, but that I may be understood. You may not have meant it for flattery but I took it as such, so if you value my friendship please do avoid flattery in every form towards me....

You say that you dare not hope that I think more of you than a common friend. No, I do not. How could you expect me to be sure there are those I have known for years that I have no kinder feelings for them nor as kind as I have for you and have denied them the request that to you I granted still I wish for no nearer tie outside of my home, than a true and warm-hearted friend. Perhaps you will ask me why it is if you do I will answer you.

You also ask if I have objections to our changing ambrotypes? I most assuredly have. That was one of the sentences which gave me pain. You may think me a queer girl – but I have several reasons for refusing that request. One is this. Our acquaintance has been very short. But do not think that I deem that a sufficient reason. Far from it. If you had heard the low vulgar expressions I once heard uttered by a youth while gazing at a likeness of a pure minded noble girl, you would not wonder that I then made a vow to never let my portrait go into the hands of a gentleman when he was nothing more than a common friend. Do not imagine that I think you would be guilty of such a base act. No, never. If I did Addie would be the wrong one to be writing to you now. But that vow is made and cannot be broken. I think that where a gentleman and lady are engaged, then they should change portraits. For then it is a sacred gift but not till then.

Now you have my reasons in full. . . .

Yours in friendship

Addie Case

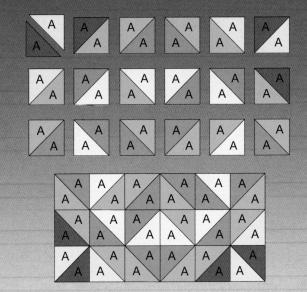

BLOCK 1
All Hallows
Adelaide

6" finished
Fabrics required: Cream 3, Cream 4, Red 1, Red 2
and Green 5

Cutting

From the Cream 3, cut:
* 6 – 1 7/8" squares. Cut each once on the diagonal to yield 12 triangles.

From the Cream 4, cut:
* 4 - 1 7/8" squares. Cut each once on the diagonal to yield 8 triangles.

From the Red 1, cut:
* 4 – 1 7/8" squares. Cut each once on the diagonal to yield 8 triangles.

From the Red 2, cut:
* 10 – 1 7/8" squares. Cut each once on the diagonal to yield 20 triangles.

From the Green 5, cut:
* 12 – 1 7/8" squares. Cut each once on the diagonal to yield 24 triangles.

Piecing

Half-square triangle units
* Units are 1" finished. Press to the dark.
* Sew 4 Cream 4 triangles to 4 Red 1 triangles.
* Sew 4 Red 1 triangles to 4 Green 5 triangles.
* Sew 12 Green 5 triangles to 12 Red 2.
* Sew 4 Cream 4 triangles to 4 Green 5 triangles.
* Sew 4 Green 5 triangles to 4 Cream 3 triangles.
* Sew 8 Cream 3 triangles to 8 Red 2 triangles.

Block Assembly

Referring to the diagram lay out the half-square triangle units in 6 rows of 6 units each. Sew the units together alternating the pressing direction with each row so your seams will nestle as you join your rows. Lay out the 6 rows and sew together.

Finishing the block

Refer to the instructions on page 66 and make the pieced setting for the All Hallows block. The block will measure 25 1/2" finished.

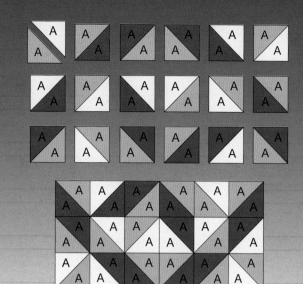

BLOCK 1

All Hallows

Charlie

6" finished
Fabric required: Cream 1, Blue 1 and Brown 1

Cutting

From the Cream 1, cut:
* 10 - 1 7/8" squares. Cut each once on the diagonal to yield 20 triangles.

From the Blue 1, cut:
* 14 - 1 7/8" squares. Cut each one on the diagonal to yield 28 triangles.

From the Brown 1, cut:
* 12 – 1 7/8" squares. Cut each once on the diagonal to yield 24 triangles.

Piecing

Half-square triangle units
* Units are 1" finished. Press to the dark
* Sew 12 Blue triangles to 12 Cream triangles.
* Sew 16 Blue triangles to 16 Brown triangles.
* Sew 8 Brown triangles to 8 Cream triangles.

Block Assembly

Referring to the diagram lay out the half-square triangle units in 6 rows of 6 units each. Sew the units together alternating the pressing direction with each row so your seams will nestle as you join your rows. Lay out the 6 rows and sew together.

Finishing the block

Refer to the instructions on page 68 and make the pieced setting for the All Hallows block. The block will measure 18" finished.

CHAPTER 2

After Addie told Charles that she would not send him her photo, she grew concerned as the weeks passed and he did not reply. Addie learned that his regiment had left its base camp in Ohio and feared her letter did not reach him. She sent a follow-up on August 10 explaining that she had learned his regiment was now stationed in Virginia and hoped he was doing well.

A month passes and still Addie has no word from Charles. Then, she hears that his unit has been in combat. Addie fears for his safety as well as the safety of her own brother, Hallie, who is initially listed as deceased in the local paper. Describing her reaction, she comments:

> I was almost surprised not to have received a letter from you immediately after the fight. I felt very anxious to hear and we did not receive a letter from Hal until yesterday. In fact his death came in the papers. It was soon contradicted but suspense is almost as bad as reality."

She concludes by pleading for some response from Charles:

> If you can write immediately after receiving this please do so.
>
> Yours in friendship,
>
> Addie Case

Finally, on September 16, Charlie posts a letter describing his daily life:

> Dear Friend Addie,
>
> War has its vicissitudes as well as the other phases of life and they are not a few I'll assure you. For the past few weeks things have been constantly changing; one day we would be reposing in perceived security and perhaps the next morning be awakened and moved to haste to prepare to meet the meet the enemy who were momentarily expected to come upon us. . . .

> I had no idea of the feelings produced by being engaged in a battle until the fight at Cross Lanes. These feelings were indescribable. I had no thoughts of dodging the balls nor did I think of getting killed. All I did was to take one thought of friends (including you, my dear Addie) then watch for an opportunity to send some "Secesh" to "Kingdom Come." But although we saw them on our front, right, and left, I thought I would reserve my fire till I was sure of my man, or at least till the order was given to fire so lost a chance to discharge my piece. . . .

Charlie continues his letter with detailed descriptions of how well Addie's brother, Hal, conducted himself during battle. He closes by encouraging Addie to keep up her correspondence:

> "Write soon Addie and a good long letter. Your letters are so good and entertaining. I love them. Give my respects to Laurie and all to whom you see fit and believe me
>
> I remain, sincerely and ever yours,
>
> Charlie

Charlie and Addie continue their light-hearted correspondence over the next two months and then Addie reveals that perhaps her feelings run deeper than she has let on in a letter dated October 16, 1861:

> How is your health now dear Charlie? You must be very careful and prudent in regard to your health for if I should learn that you were ill I should so long to be with you and supply your wants and you know that it would not be very convenient if you was way down in Charleston.

She closes the letter by revealing a bit more of her feelings:

> The Good Bye lingers but I must give it. Please write soon to your "Ohio Sister,"
>
> Addie,
>
> Heavens choicest blessings be thine dear Charlie, involuntarily escapes from the lips of Addie.

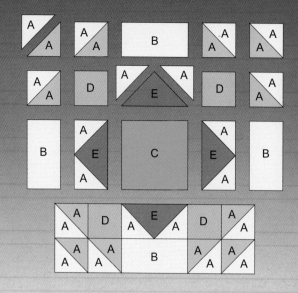

Summer Wind

Adelaide

6" finished
Fabrics required: Cream 1, Red 1, Green 1, Green 5 and Brown 2

Cutting

From the Cream 1, cut:

* 10 – 1 7/8" squares. Cut each once on the diagonal to yield 20 A triangles.

* 4 – 1 1/2" x 2 1/2" B rectangles.

From the Red 1, cut:

* 1 - 3 1/4" square. Cut on both diagonals to yield 4 E triangles.

From the Green 1, cut:

* 1 – 2 1/2" C square.

From the Green 5, cut:

* 6 - 1 7/8" squares. Cut each once on the diagonal to yield 12 A triangles.

From the Brown 2, cut:

* 4 – 1 1/2" D squares.

Piecing

Half-square triangle units

* Units are 1" finished. Press to the dark.

* Sew 12 Cream 1 A triangles to 12 Green 5 A triangles to make 12 half-square triangles.

Flying geese units

* Units are 1" x 2" finished.

* Sew 2 Cream 1 A triangles to both sides of a Red 1 E triangle. Press to the A triangles. Make 4.

Block Assembly

Referring to the diagram lay out the half-square triangle units, rectangles, flying geese units and squares in 5 rows. Sew the units together pressing toward the B, C and D squares. Lay out the 5 rows and sew together.

Finishing the block

Refer to the instructions on page 66 and make the pieced setting for the Summer Wind block. The block will measure 25 1/2" finished.

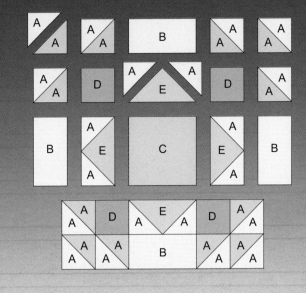

Summer Wind

Charlie

6" finished

Fabrics required: Cream 2, Blue 2, Blue 3 and Brown 2

Cutting

From the Cream 2, cut:

* 10 – 1 7/8" squares. Cut each once on the diagonal to yield 20 A triangles.

* 4 – 1 1/2" x 2 1/2" B rectangles.

From the Blue 2, cut:

* 1 – 3 1/4" square. Cut on both diagonals to yield 4 E triangles.

From the Blue 3, cut:

* 4 – 1 1/2" D squares.

From the Brown 2, cut:

* 6 – 1 7/8" squares. Cut each once on the diagonal to yield 12 A triangles.

* 1 – 2 1/2" C square.

Piecing

Half-square triangle units

* Units are 1" finished. Press to the dark.

* Sew 12 Cream 2 A triangles to 12 Brown 2 A triangles to make 12 half-square triangles.

Flying geese units

* Units are 1" x 2" finished.

* Sew 2 Cream 2 A triangles to both sides of a Blue 2 E triangle. Press to the A triangles. Make 4.

Block Assembly

Referring to the diagram lay out the half-square triangle units, rectangles, flying geese units and squares in 5 rows. Sew the units together pressing toward the B, C and D squares. Lay out the 5 rows and sew together.

Finishing the block

Refer to the instructions on page 68 and make the pieced setting for the Summer Wind block. The block will measure 18" finished.

CHAPTER 3

Perhaps emboldened by Addie's flirtations of mid-October, Charlie moves forward in his courtship of Adelaide in his October 24 letter:

My dearest Addie,

I commenced to say, involuntarily too, dearest Addie. Would it have been right? You would not have remonstrated would you? And then it is just the way I feel anyhow. Your sweet little letter of the 12th I received yesterday morning and you can imagine if you can with what joy and pleasure I read it. Perhaps you can form some idea of the longing and impatience with which I watch the arrival of the mails for a letter from Addie, when I tell you that Addie is the only correspondent I have. Now you don't wonder why I want you to write often, do you?

But, I flatter myself (not you,) that I have the prettiest and best correspondent, that soldiers "or any other man" commonly have. That I feel that I am worthy of your kind attention, but I love to have some one to whom I can turn and know and feel that it is indeed a friend. Such I believe my Addie to be.

Do not think I mean to flatter you, for it is the truth, and then you told me not to try to flatter you, and I won't do what you don't want me to. 'Twas a happy day for me when I saw you first. . . .

I am on guard today and am now momentarily expecting to hear "First Relief, fall in." then comes two long hours of steady marching up and down a long "beat." But then after that I have four hours rest. The regiment is out on Battalion drill, in front of the camp, on our parade ground.

The boys have become very efficient in drill. It is not as easy to "form close column of attack on fifth company" while on double quick time, as it was to "change front on sixth company" while in Camp Dennison. But of course you do not know what those commands mean, so I will stop talking Military. You should see us on dress Parade; and see what a neat appearance we present. There is to be dress Parade this afternoon at 3-oclock. How I wish you could be here to see us. Our camp is situated two miles up from Charleston, and is a very beautiful camp indeed. Our Regiment is now all here and our band too. I do not know when we can get furlough. Nor does Hal. When he comes, though we cannot tell when it will be, I will probably comply with your request and come with him.

I remain yours affectionately and forever,

Charlie

Then, in an apparent nod to Addie's shyness and virtue, he adds a post-script which he only half-heartedly crosses out. Clearly, his intent is that she sees that he wrote:

P.S. Would you accept a kiss; if I were to enclose one? Burn this up won't you?

THE YOUNG VOLUNTEER.
"BULLY FOR YOU"

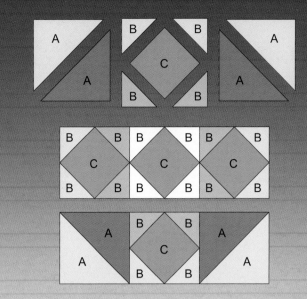

BLOCK 3

❧ *Sawtooth* ❧

Adelaide

6" finished

Fabrics required: Cream 1, Cream 2, Red 1, Red 4 and Brown 2

Cutting

From the Cream 1, cut:

* 2 – 2 7/8" squares. Cut each once on the diagonal to yield 4 A triangles.

* 4 – 1 7/8" squares. Cut each once on the diagonal to yield 8 B triangles.

From the Cream 2, cut:

* 2 – 1 7/8" squares. Cut each once on the diagonal to yield 4 B triangles.

From the Red 1, cut:

* 5 – 1 7/8" C squares.

From the Red 4, cut:

* 2 – 2 7/8" squares. Cut each once on the diagonal to yield 4 A triangles.

From the Brown 2, cut:

* 4 – 1 7/8" squares. Cut each once on the diagonal to yield 8 B triangles.

Piecing

Half-square triangle units

* Units are 2" finished. Press to the dark.

* Sew a Cream 1 A triangle to a Red 4 A triangle. Make 4.

Square-in-a-square units

* Units are 2" finished.

* Sew 2 Brown 2 B triangles to adjoining edges of a Red 1 C square. Press to the triangles. Sew 2 Cream 1 B triangles to opposite adjoining sides of the Red 1 C square. Press to the triangles. Make 4.

* Sew 4 Cream 2 B triangles to each edge of the remaining Red 1 C square. Press to the triangles. Make 1.

Block Assembly

Referring to the diagram lay out the half-square triangle units and square-in-a-square units in 3 rows of 3 units. Sew the rows together, making sure the square-in-a-square units are facing the correct direction and alternating the pressing directions with each row so your seams will nestle as you join your rows. Lay out the 3 rows and sew together.

Finishing the block

Refer to the instructions on page 66 and make the pieced setting for the Sawtooth block. The block will measure 25 1/2" finished.

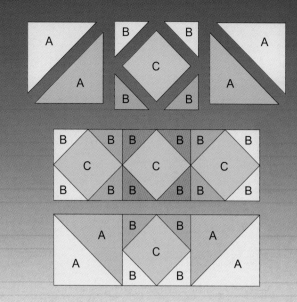

BLOCK 3

❦ *Sawtooth* ❦

Charlie

6" finished

Fabrics required: Cream 5, Blue 1, Blue 3, Brown 1 and Brown 2

Cutting

From the Cream 5, cut:

* 2 – 2 7/8" squares. Cut each once on the diagonal to yield 4 A triangles.

* 4 – 1 7/8" squares. Cut each once on the diagonal to yield 8 B triangles.

From the Blue 1, cut:

* 5 – 1 7/8" C squares.

From the Blue 3, cut:

* 4 – 1 7/8" squares. Cut each once on the diagonal to yield 8 B triangles.

From the Brown 1, cut:

* 2 – 1 7/8" squares. Cut each once on the diagonal to yield 4 B triangles.

From the Brown 2, cut:

* 2 – 2 7/8" squares. Cut each once on the diagonal to yield 4 A triangles.

Piecing

Half-square triangle units

* Units are 2" finished. Press to the dark.

* Sew a Cream 5 A triangle to a Brown 2 A triangle. Make 4.

Square-in-a-square units

* Units are 2" finished.

* Sew 2 Blue 3 B triangles to adjoining edges of a Blue 1 C square. Press to the triangles. Sew 2 Cream 5 B triangles to opposite adjoining sides of the Blue 1 C square. Press to the triangles. Make 4.

* Sew 4 Brown 1 B triangles to each edge of the remaining Blue 1 C square. Press to the triangles. Make 1.

Block Assembly

Referring to the diagram lay out the half-square triangle units and square-in-a-square units in 3 rows of 3 units. Sew the rows together, making sure the square-in-a-square units are facing the correct direction and alternating the pressing directions with each row so your seams will nestle as you join your rows. Lay out the 3 rows and sew together.

Finishing the block

Refer to the instructions on page 68 and make the pieced setting for the Sawtooth block. The block will measure 18" finished.

CHAPTER 4

The next documented correspondence between Addie and Charles occurred in December, 1861. On December 7, Addie writes to describe an attempt at courtship from a local man, James Beebe:

"Dear to Charlie,

Do you not think I should be thankful for the long list of letters I have received from Mr. Tenney during the past two months? Have you not written to me? . . . If Hal had not been with you I should have thought you was ill . . . .

Oh, Charlie I had some sport the other evening. James Beebe came here. I was busily reading one of Hal's letters when I heard a rather timid rap on the door. I arose and opened when who should appear but said Beebe. I seated a chair for him and resumed my reading – you know how I detest him. He hemmed a few times took his hat and laid on the floor then drew his chair near the table and took up an ambrotype, which he had seen time after time. But he must do something I presume he felt more like a man with that before him than waiting in awkward silence for me to make a move. But not long did he wait. I arose with "Do you wish to see my father? I will call him" and stepped toward the door. "Ahem Miss Addie," he stammered out, I turned. "I–I thought I'd call and see if you'd let me stay with you a little while" he at last said. I told him – well guess what? At that moment he heard father coming toward the door when he sprang and went out like a deer, leaving me so convulsed with laughter that it was some time after father came in before I could explain to him. . . ."

After recounting her teasing of Mr. Beebe, Addie goes on to describe a lecture by a visiting missionary which she attended:

"And thus I compared them with the vast numbers of slaves held in subjugation in my own country. This beautiful America! It was then I prayed that this war might never close until our land should be freed from the curse of slavery. . . . How many noble sentiments are cherished in the heart which are never brought to light, because the energy necessary to carry them into effect is wanting. A few untoward circumstances are enough to dampen the zeal and put an end to the finest suggestions. . . .

You will write as soon as you receive this won't you dear friend? I get so anxious to hear from you.

My kind regards to those I know.

Love to Hal.

Yours in friendship.

Addie

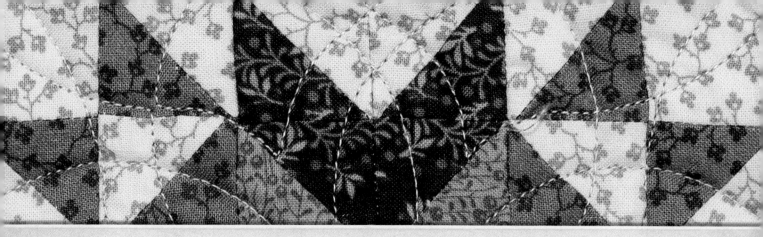

While Addie was composing this letter, Charles was busy writing his own missive to Adelaide dated December 3, 1861:

> Dearest Addie,
>
> I owe you more than a simple apology for neglecting to write the sweetest being God ever made (I am not flattering, my heart tells me so) but perhaps your throne of beauty may be a throne of mercy and its occupant may perchance be lenient toward and humble subjects and forgive me for this time.
>
> But, dear Addie, I will strive hereafter to be more punctual. It is not because I did not wish to write that I have not sooner answered your letters and acknowledge edge the receipt of your beautiful present, but for reasons which are in themselves "cogent," as a lawyer would say, (Now is that the word? I saw it used in that way anyhow.)
>
> The weather has been very severe, for the past-few, weeks, (the boys are making such an uproar I can scarcely concentrate my thoughts) and we are still in our thin summer tents and we are rather crowded. Imagine how twelve men would occupy the little room in which I staid at your home and you can have an idea of our situation. . . .
>
> I will try to win your lasting favor. You called yourself my "Ohio Sister." Indeed Addie, you are, anymore than sister and I hope to prove myself self worthy of a sister's love. May I hope for it?

Charles goes on to describe his opinions about various changes in the military and its command. Unfortunately, this letter ends abruptly as it appears the last page or pages are missing.

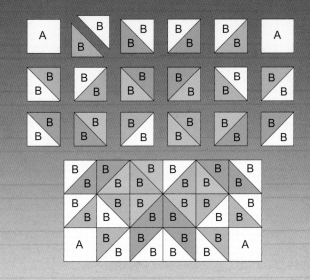

Wyoming Valley
Adelaide

6" finished

Fabrics required: Cream 3, Red 3, Green 1 and Green 4

Cutting

From the Cream 3, cut:

* 4 – 1 1/2" A squares.

* 11 – 1 7/8" squares. Cut each once on the diagonal to yield 22 B triangles.

From the Red 3, cut:

* 8 – 1 7/8" squares. Cut each once on the diagonal to yield 16 B triangles.

From the Green 1, cut:

* 8 – 1 7/8" squares Cut each once on the diagonal to yield 16 B triangles.

From the Green 4, cut:

* 5 – 1 7/8" squares. Cut each once on the diagonal to yield 10 B triangles.

Piecing

Half-square triangle units

* Units are 1" finished. Press to the dark.

* Sew 14 Cream 3 triangles to 14 Red 3 triangles.

* Sew 8 Cream 3 triangles to 8 Green 1 triangles.

* Sew 8 Green 1 triangles to 8 Green 4 triangles.

* Sew 2 Green 4 triangles to 2 Red 3 triangles.

Block Assembly

Referring to the diagram lay out the half-square triangle units and squares in 6 rows of 6 units each. Sew the row together, pressing each row to the opposite side. Lay out the 6 rows and sew together.

Finishing the block

Refer to the instructions on page 66 and make the pieced setting for the Wyoming Valley block. The block will measure 25 1/2" finished.

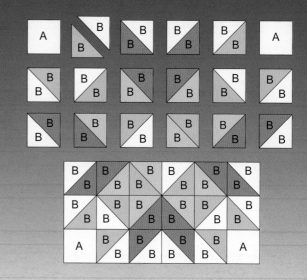

Wyoming Valley
Charlie

6" finished

Fabrics required: Cream 3, Blue 2, Brown 2 and Brown 3

Cutting

From the Cream 3, cut:

- ✳ 4 – 1 1/2" A squares.
- ✳ 11 – 1 7/8" squares. Cut each once on the diagonal to yield 22 B triangles.

From the Blue 2, cut:

- ✳ 8 – 1 7/8" squares. Cut each once on the diagonal to yield 16 B triangles.

From the Brown 2, cut:

- ✳ 5 – 1 7/8" squares. Cut each once on the diagonal to yield 10 B triangles.

From the Brown 3, cut:

- ✳ 8 – 1 7/8" squares. Cut each once on the diagonal to yield 16 B triangles.

Piecing

Half-square triangle units

- ✳ Units are 1" finished. Press to the dark.
- ✳ Sew 14 Cream 3 triangles to 14 Blue 2 triangles.
- ✳ Sew 8 Cream 3 triangles to 8 Brown 3 triangles.
- ✳ Sew 8 Brown 3 triangles to 8 Brown 2 triangles.
- ✳ Sew 2 Blue 2 triangles to 2 Brown 2 triangles.

Block Assembly

Referring to the diagram lay out the half-square triangle units and squares in 6 rows of 6 units each. Sew the rows together, pressing each row to the opposite side. Lay out the 6 rows and sew together.

Finishing the block

Refer to the instructions on page 68 and make the pieced setting for the Wyoming Valley block. The block will measure 18" finished.

CHAPTER 5

By December 11, 1861, Charlie is on his way to Virginia with his unit.

My dear Addie,

My health is good, how is yours Addie, dear? How glad I am that writing was invented long ago, and that I have a good memory, for I seem to see you, sitting by your sweet toned melodeon, your soul giving utterance to its goodness in happy song, the music of which seems to reach me, and enliven my inmost spirit. How glad am I, to know and feel that you are at this moment holding me in kind remembrance. Happiness is a boon many strive to reach, but few comparatively attain, but if happiness exists among soldiers, it is him, who knows that there is a heart which beats in unison with his own, and feels that her spirit is watching over him, that is the fortunate possessor.

Am I mistaken in believing that here is one who thus remembers me, and that one, Addie? Forgive me if do wrong in thus plainly expressing myself, for it is the promptings of my heart, and my conscience reproves me often for not doing as I ought. I speak thus to hush its reproving voice. But, although our acquaintance has been short, has it been productive of ill? Has your heart not been moved in unison with mine? But I'll bide my time, perhaps I may meet you again. Forgive me if I have done wrong.

In a few short hours, we leave the pleasant view of Ohio, and retreat to the wilds of Virginia, perhaps never to return, for I learn by the way that we are to enter the field again. If I fall, I fall in the defense of my once happy country. I shall die "unwept, unhonored, and unknown." But of this, in the main, I care not, all I wish to know is that if I fall I shall be regretted by one. Assured that such is the case, I die happy. . . .

Your true

Charlie

Charlie continued his correspondence as he moved across Virginia. On December 13, he wrote:

My dear friend,

Lest you toss all knowledge of our whereabouts, I again send you a few lines. We are well and in good spirits, but as yet uncertain as to where we shall be sent. . . .

Charlie goes on to describe his journey by train into Virginia and describes the living conditions:

Now dear Addie, imagine yourself a soldier jolted along for hundreds of miles in a cold uncomfortable freight car, night and day, and then when you stopped be obliged to lie wherever you could perchance in a cold corner of a car, or perhaps "en bivouack" by the side of a fire which you must often replenish, or freeze. Suppose for a moment you were there situated and you have some idea of our way of living. We are now without tents but expecting new ones every day. . . .

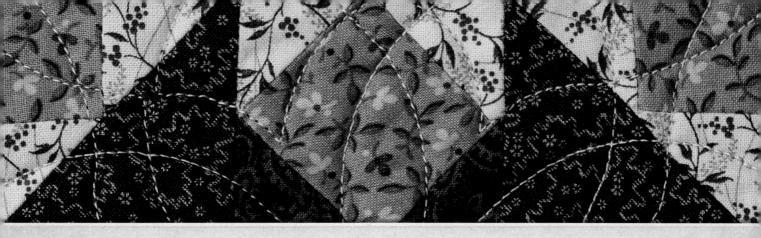

I would like to see you now. I suppose you have sleighing now, do you not? Please take one ride for me, will you not? And be happy and joyous as you can. I know you remember me for I seem to feel your presence every day and night. I never felt happier in my life than since I knew you loved me well enough to style yourself my sister; am I worthy of being called a brother?

What do you think of the movements of Gen. McClellan? Is his policy one of those brilliant actions which characterized the first Napoleon? And Gen. Halleck, too? What do you think of his grand withdrawal of troops from central Missouri? Perhaps though, as Price's plan is to remove the field to Kansas. Halleck wishes to lure him back to Missouri, and severely whip him but he is not Fremont. . . .

When you write, please write me a good long letter and remember you are writing to one who loves you dearly, and would if necessary die for you.

I must now bid you farewell for the present.

Remaining yours forever,

Charlie Tenney

Gen'l Robert Anderson

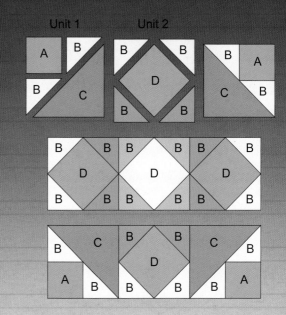

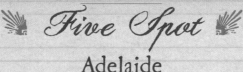

Five Spot

Adelaide

6" finished

Fabrics required: Cream 2, Red 2, Red 5, Green 2 and Green 3

Cutting

From the Cream 2, cut:

* 8 – 1 7/8" squares. Cut each once on the diagonal to yield 16 B triangles.
* 1 – 1 7/8" D square.

From the Red 2, cut:

* 4 – 1 1/2" A squares.
* 4 – 1 7/8" D squares.

From the Red 5, cut:

* 2 – 2 7/8" squares. Cut each once on the diagonal to yield 4 C triangles.

From the Green 2, cut:

* 2 – 1 7/8" squares. Cut each once on the diagonal to yield 4 B triangles.

From the Green 3, cut:

* 4 – 1 7/8" squares. Cut each once on the diagonal to yield 8 B triangles.

Piecing

Unit 1

* Units are 2" finished.

* Sew 2 Cream 2 B triangles to either side of a Red 2 A square. Press to the triangles. Sew a Red 5 C triangle to this unit to make a square. Make 4.

Unit 2

Square-in-a-square units

* Units are 2" finished.

* Sew 2 Cream 2 B triangles to adjoining edges of a Red 2 D square. Press to the triangles. Sew 2 Green 3 B triangles to opposite, adjoining sides of the Red 2 D square. Press to the triangles. Make 4.

* Sew 4 Green 2 B triangles to each edge of a Cream 2 D square. Press to the triangles. Make 1.

Block Assembly

Referring to the diagram lay out the Unit 1 squares and Unit 2 squares in 3 rows of 3 units. Sew the rows together, making sure the Unit 1 squares are facing the correct direction and alternating the pressing directions with each row so your seams will nestle as you join your rows. Lay out the 3 rows and sew together.

Finishing the block

Refer to the instructions on page 66 and make the pieced setting for the Five Spot block. The block will measure 25 1/2" finished.

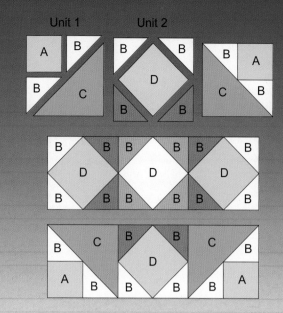

Five Spot
Charlie

6" finished

Fabrics required: Cream 5, Blue 1, Blue 3, Blue 6 and Brown 1

Cutting

From the Cream 5, cut:

* 8 – 1 7/8" squares. Cut each once on the diagonal to yield 16 B triangles.

* 1 – 1 7/8" D square.

From the Blue 1, cut:

* 4 – 1 1/2" A squares.

* 4 – 1 7/8" D squares.

From the Blue 3, cut:

* 2 – 1 7/8" squares. Cut each once on the diagonal to yield 4 B triangles

From the Blue 6, cut:

* 2 – 2 7/8" squares. Cut each once on the diagonal to yield 4 C triangles

From the Brown 1, cut:

* 4 – 1 7/8" squares. Cut each once on the diagonal to yield 8 B triangles

Piecing

Unit 1

* Units are 2" finished.

* Sew 2 Cream 5 B triangles to either side of a Blue 1 A square. Press to the triangles. Sew a Blue 6 C triangle to this unit to make a square. Make 4.

Unit 2

Square-in-a-square units

* Units are 2" finished.

* Sew 2 Cream 5 B triangles to adjoining edges of a Blue 1 D square. Press to the triangles. Sew 2 Brown 1 B triangles to opposite, adjoining sides of the Cream 5 D square. Press to the triangles. Make 4.

* Sew 4 Blue 3 B triangles to each edge of a Cream 5 D square. Press to the triangles. Make 1.

Block Assembly

Referring to the diagram lay out the Unit1 squares and Unit 2 squares in 3 rows of 3 units. Sew the rows together, making sure the Unit 1 squares are facing the correct direction and alternating the pressing directions with each row so your seams will nestle as you join your rows. Lay out the 3 rows and sew together.

Finishing the block

Refer to the instructions on page 68 and make the pieced setting for the Five Spot block. The block will measure 18" finished.

CHAPTER 6

As the New Year dawned, Charlie still had not received any reply from Adelaide, however he continued to write her, composing two separate letters on January 1, 1862. In both, he expresses his hope for the New Year and his appreciation for Addie.

In the first letter of the day Charlie reports on her brother, Hal's, health and wishes her well.

A happy new year to you dear.

To: Addie, and my kindest wishes in your interest.

How do you do, this beautiful day? Did you ever see such a beautiful new year's day in your life? The day here is as pleasant as the most delightful day I ever saw in May.

The main things wanted though, to make me perfectly happy to-day, are, first a letter from my Addie, second Hal's recovery from his present indisposition. He has not been well for the past few days and last night he was some worse, but is, I trust, better this morning I hope he will soon be able to resume his duties. He is not so bad however, as to call in the Doctor yet, and I hope will not.

I have received but one letter since we left Charleston, and that one was sent to Charleston first. In it you spoke of not receiving a letter from me since Capt. Asper returned. Have you not received any of the letters I have written? I sent one from Charleston, one from Parkersburg, one from Green Spring Run, and two from Romney together with a picture of "yours truly" I have been waiting for Wood to return hoping he would bring me some tidings from you, but he does not come, and as I went in and saw Hal, he asked me to write home and let you know he was unwell, so

I add one more to the list of unanswered letters.

I was on picket the other day and had a first rate time. . . . There is a peculiar sort of excitement in standing on picket guard that I love. One takes his post in the evening, banishes all though of comfort rest, and gives way to his own thoughts, all the time on the quiver, expecting to hear the click of a gun lock, the step of an enemy, or, perchance, the discharge of a gun itself, summoning him to another world. The rustling of the breeze through the dry leaves, (for there is no snow) or the cry of some night bird calling for its mate makes him involuntarily get his gun in readiness to meet the expected foe.

Sometimes it happens that inefficient men are placed on a dangerous post, as on the last night I stood. A man was placed on a post near mine, and towards daylight he fancied he saw a man preparing to make a hostile movement. Frightened nearly to death, he drew up his musket and fired. An alarm was thus raised needlessly. In the morning, we visited the spot where the supposed had stood, when lo, a bush appeared, having seen it move he shot it. . . .

Do write soon dear Addie, for I am so lonesome.

Yours as ever

Charlie

Later in the day, Charlie was compelled to write again.

"My dear friend,

Although I have once written to day, duty and my own inclination lead me to pen a few more scattered thoughts to my dearest, kindest friend.

To: Addie

Now, to speak truly, I feel more like myself to-night than this morning, for two reasons, which reasons, are the fulfillment of my two wishes expressed in my note of this morning. The reception of a letter from you and about Hal's getting better. He is some better tonight, though not well. The wind has been blowing very hard, all day, and the tent kept flapping and making a very disagreeable noise to Hal. Consequently, a severe headache ensued, but the gale has in a measure subsided, and I trust a good night's rest will restore him to his wanted good health. But to turn to other subjects. Have you passed a happy new year's day? And did your thoughts revert once to "Soldier boy" Charlie? And wonder if he was engaged in some Bechanalian excesses? . . ."

Charlie then recounts how over the course of the past few weeks he was decided to refrain from using both alcohol and tobacco and avoid playing cards. He hopes these decisions will please Adelaide, explaining why he made them:

I did for my own benefit and character hereafter. Is Addie satisfied with this statement? It is I believe the truth. Oh! the temptations of a soldier's life! How great the want of some restraining influence at home! "Home," Tears involuntarily spring to my yes as I utter that endearing word, and think. "I have no home." But fate has decreed that one remains, not too proud to own an outcast soldier as a brother.

That you should find anything worthy a sister's love in my poor self, is a matter of wonder to me. How can I ever repay you for your kindness in noticing one so far below your happy position? But, do I wound you? Forgive me dear, kind sister, and I will endeavor to dispel the unpleasant state of mind, which has come over me in a few moments of bitter thought.

This letter trails off with some description of the encampment but lacks any closing which suggests the remainder of the letter was lost or destroyed.

BLOCK 6

Auntie's Chain

Adelaide

6" finished

Fabrics required: Cream 3, Red 1, Green 1, Green 2, Green 3 and Green 5

Cutting

From the Cream 3, cut:

* 4 – 3 1/4" squares. Cut each on both diagonals to yield 16 A triangles. (You will only use 14 in the piecing.)

From the Red 1, cut:

* 1 – 3 1/4" square. Cut on both diagonals to yield 4 A triangles. (You will only use 2 in the piecing).

* 2 – 1 7/8" B squares.

From the Green 1, cut:

* 1 – 3 1/4" square. Cut on both diagonals to yield 4 A triangles

From the Green 2, cut:

* 1 – 3 1/4" square. Cut on both diagonals to yield 4 A triangles.

From the Green 3, cut:

* 2 – 1 7/8" B squares.

From the Green 5, cut:

* 1 – 3 1/4" square. Cut on both diagonals to yield 4 A triangles.

Piecing

Four-patch unit

* Unit is 2 3/4" finished.

* Make a four-patch unit for the center of the block using 2 Green 3 B squares and 2 Red 1 B squares. Press to the dark.

Half-square triangle units

* Units are 1 3/8" finished. Press to the dark.

* Sew a Cream 3 A triangle to a Green 5. Make 4.

* Sew a Cream 3 A triangle to a Green 1. Make 2.

* Sew a Cream 3 A triangle to a Red 1. Make 2.

* Referring to the diagram for placement, sew a Red 1 half-square triangle to a Green 5 half-square triangle. Press to the green. Make 2.

* Sew a Green 1 half-square triangle to a Green 5 half-square triangle. Press to the Green 5. Make 2

Triangle units

❋ Sew the short side of a Green 2 triangle to the short side of a Cream 3 triangle. Press to the green. Make 2.

❋ Sew the short side of a Green 2 triangle to the short side of a Cream 3 triangle. Make sure this is a mirror image of the first 2 units. Press to the green. Make 2.

Block Assembly

Side sections

❋ Referring to the diagram for color placement, sew a Green 1 and a Cream 3 triangle to either side of the Green 5/ Red 1 half square triangle unit. Press to the triangles. To the top of this unit, sew a Green 2/Cream 3 unit. Press to the Green 2/Cream 3 triangle units. Make 2.

Middle section

❋ Referring to the diagram for color placement, sew a Green 2/Cream 3 triangle unit to the top of a Green 1/ Green 5 half-square triangle unit. Press to the triangle unit. Make 2.

❋ Sew these units to either side of the four-patch unit. Press to the four-patch.

❋ Lay out the two side sections and middle section and sew together.

Finishing the block

Refer to the instructions on page 66 and make the pieced setting for the Auntie's Chain block. The block will measure 25 1/2" finished.

❧ *Auntie's Chain* ❧
Charlie

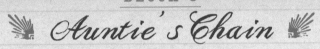

6" finished

Fabrics required: Cream 3, Cream 5, Blue 2, Blue 3, Blue 5 and Brown 1

Cutting

From the Cream 3, cut:

* 4 – 3 1/4" squares. Cut each on both diagonals to yield 16 A triangles. (You will use only 14 in the piecing.)

From the Cream 5, cut:

* 2 – 1 7/8" B squares.

From the Blue 2, cut:

* 1 – 3 1/4" square. Cut on both diagonals to yield 4 A triangles.

From the Blue 3, cut:

* 1 – 3 1/4" square. Cut on both diagonals to yield 4 A triangles.

From the Blue 5, cut:

* 1 – 3 1/4" square. Cut on both diagonals to yield 4 A triangles. (You will use only 2 in the piecing.)

* 2 – 1 7/8" B squares.

From the Brown 1, cut:

* 1 – 3 1/4" square. Cut on both diagonals to yield 4 A triangles.

Piecing

Four-patch unit

* Unit is 2 3/4" finished.

* Make a four-patch unit for the center of the block using 2 Blue 5 B squares and 2 Cream 5 B squares. Press to the dark.

Half-square triangle units

* Units are 1 3/8" finished. Press to the dark.

* Sew a Cream 3 A triangle to a Blue 2. Make 4.

* Sew a Cream 3 A triangle to a Brown 1. Make 2.

* Sew a Cream 3 A triangle to a Blue 5. Make 2.

* Referring to the diagram for placement, sew a Brown 1 half-square triangle to a Blue 2 half-square triangle. Press to the blue. Make 2.

* Sew a Blue 5 half-square triangle to a Blue 2 half-square triangle. Press to the Blue 2. Make 2

Triangle units

✳ Sew the short side of a Blue 3 triangle to the short side of a Cream 3 triangle. Press to the blue. Make 2.

✳ Sew the short side of a Blue 3 triangle to the short side of a Cream 3 triangle. Make sure this is a mirror image of the first 2 units. Press to the blue. Make 2.

Block Assembly

Side sections

✳ Referring to the diagram for color placement, sew a Brown 1 and a Cream 3 triangle to either side of the Blue 5/Blue 2 half square triangle unit. Press to the triangles. To the top of this unit, sew a Blue 3/Cream 3 unit. Press to the Blue 3/Cream 3 triangles. Make 2.

Middle section

✳ Referring to the diagram for color placement, sew a Blue 3/Cream 3 triangle unit to the top of a Blue 2/Brown 1 half-square triangle unit. Press to the triangle unit. Make 2.

✳ Sew these units to either side of the four-patch unit. Press to the four-patch.

✳ Lay out the two side sections and middle section and sew together.

Finishing the block

Refer to the instructions on page 68 and make the pieced setting for the Auntie's Chain block. The block will measure 18" finished.

CHAPTER 7

s **Charlie** struggled through New Year's Day, writing two letters to Adelaide, she was hard at work on her own letter that day.

Dear brother Charlie,

Here you sit right before me and now for a good long conversation. I received your welcome gift yesterday. I can assure you that it was a very acceptable Christmas gift. I can thank you much better when I see you than now.

I was awakened last night at twelve o'clock by the church bell giving notice that the "old years'" last moments had passed and the New Year had stepped into existence. Dear Charlie, you can not conceive my thoughts as I listened to the sound of that old church bell reverberating in the stillness of the night. I thought can it be that this loved country, our own country, must commence another year with the clash of arms and the cries and groans of the downtrodden resounding through the land? I would that this land could have commenced the year of 1862 in peace and true Liberty but it was otherwise willed Dear brother I sometimes tremble and entertain vague prortentions [premonitions] for your safety. But a feeble effort so made to commend you to Him who alone can rescue Life under the most auspicious circumstances is uncertain but how fearfully uncertain it must be when all the destructive powers of warfare are brought against it. But I trust that you will live to return to your friends.

. . . What a windy day this is. It seems that the elements as well as our nation were in a fierce combat with each other. But I have not time to write much more to day. You write that you receive no letters from me. I think it very strange for I may safely say that I have written weekly.

Please write soon and often.

As ever your sister

Addie

Addie writes more letters in early January describing her daily activities, but one on January 12 is especially poignant as it describes her feelings about the war.

Dear Charlie,

Every day brings to view more and more the awful verge on which our loved and wretched country is trembling. Although I am ashamed to own it yet it is nevertheless true that before this awful rebellion broke out I cast no reflections upon this, our America. I only thought of it as a good and righteous government, I lived only for myself nor even dreamed that war that worst of all evils could inhabit its land and although I cannot sympathize, even now, with our country as some can and do, yet – I feel its awful effects most deeply. I sometimes think that it is more for my friends that I care than for my country. It seems natural but it may not be right. . . .

But I must close.

Please write very often to your friend and sister

Addie

BLOCK 7
Kansas Star
Adelaide

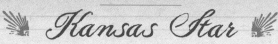

6" finished
Fabrics required: Cream 1, Cream 2, Red 5, Green 2, Green 3 and Brown 1

Cutting

From the Cream 1, cut:
* 6 – 1 7/8" squares. Cut each once on the diagonal to yield 12 A triangles.

From the Cream 2, cut:
* 2 – 1 7/8" squares. Cut each once on the diagonal to yield 4 A triangles.
* 4 – 1 7/8" B squares

From the Red 5, cut:
* 5 – 1 7/8" B squares.

From the Green 2, cut:
* 2 – 1 7/8" squares. Cut each once on the diagonal to yield 4 A triangles.

From the Green 3, cut:
* 4 – 1 7/8" squares. Cut each once on the diagonal to yield 8 A triangles.

From the Brown 1, cut:
* 4 – 1 7/8" squares. Cut each once on the diagonal to yield 8 A triangles.

Piecing

Square-in-a-square units
* Units are 2" finished. Press to the triangles.

* Sew 2 Brown 1 A triangles to adjoining edges of a Cream 2 B square. Sew 2 Green 3 A triangles to opposite adjoining sides of the B square. Make 4.

* Sew 3 Cream 1 A triangles to 3 edges of a Red 5 B square. Sew a Cream 2 A triangle to the remaining side of the square. Make 4

* Sew 4 Green 2 A triangles to each edge of a Red 5 B square. Make 1

Block Assembly

Referring to the diagram lay out the square-in-a-square units in 3 rows. Sew the units together alternating the pressing direction with each row so your seams will nestle as you join your rows. Lay out the 3 rows and sew together.

Finishing the block

Refer to the instructions on page 66 and make the pieced setting for the Kansas Star block. The block will measure 25 1/2" finished.

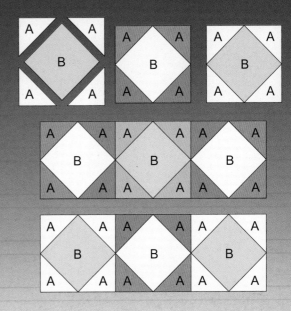

🌾 *Kansas Star* 🌾

Charlie

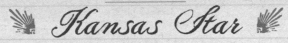

6" finished

Fabrics required: Cream 2, Blue 2, Blue 6, Brown 1 and Brown 2

Cutting

From the Cream 2, cut:

* 8 – 1 7/8" squares. Cut each once on the diagonal to yield 16 A triangles.
* 4 – 1 7/8" B squares.

From the Blue 2, cut:

* 2 – 1 7/8" squares. Cut each once on the diagonal to yield 4 A triangles.

From the Blue 6, cut:

* 4 – 1 7/8" squares. Cut each once on the diagonal to yield 8 A triangles.

From the Brown 1, cut:

* 4 – 1 7/8" squares. Cut each once on the diagonal to yield 8 A triangles.

From the Brown 2, cut:

* 5 – 1 7/8" B squares.

Piecing

Square-in-a-square units

* Units are 2" finished. Press to the triangles.

* Sew 2 Brown 1 A triangles to adjoining edges of a Cream 2 B square. Sew 2 Blue 6 A triangles to opposite adjoining sides of the B square. Make 4.

* Sew 4 Cream 2 A triangles to each edge of a Brown 2 B square. Make 4

* Sew 4 Blue 2 A triangles to each edge of a Brown 2 B square. Make 1

Block Assembly

Referring to the diagram lay out the square-in-a-square units in 3 rows. Sew the units together alternating the pressing direction with each row so your seams will nestle as you join your rows. Lay out the 3 rows and sew together.

Finishing the block

Refer to the instructions on page 68 and make the pieced setting for the Kansas Star block. The block will measure 18" finished.

CHAPTER 8

By **mid-January,** Charlie had decided to declare his true feelings for Adelaide. Over two letters, he details his devotion and affection and asks that she respond as to whether she feels the same way. On January 13, 1862, he writes:

Dear Addie,

I love you better than ever. Do not think me presumptuous. Addie if I say I love you. Do not discard me from your thoughts. I will try to make myself worthy of your love. Do I speak too assured? Hallie assures me that he has not the least objection to our correspondence, and leaves me to act as I see proper. With you, now rests my happiness. Shall I be happy or the reverse? Do you ask me to wait until you become better acquainted with me? I do not ask or expect that on so short acquaintance you shall decide forever.

May I hope to find you happy when I come home?

But I must close, or I will become tedious.

Hoping to receive a good long letter from My Addie.

I remain yours forever. (Hallie's love accompanies this.)

Charlie

Before receiving a reply from Adelaide, Charles sends another letter on January 18:

My dearest Addie,

As all is known, now, dear Addie need we have any secrets? I mean as regards the feelings predominant in our hearts. Addie, I cannot refrain from telling you all. Pardon me, I love you, Addie, not with that momentary effervescence with a pure, fervent affection, which comes welling up from my heart, all unbidden, but irresistible. It may perhaps be wrong – you are far above me, in worth and position – but my love is from the heart, and increases in strength daily. Addie is in my thoughts by night and by day. But for thy darling letters, and the impression on my heart when I saw you – I might have become demoralized and lost forever. Addie, do I love in vain? Do my feelings meet with no response in your heart? With you, dear Addie rests my future. Will it be a happy one, happy in your love or must I be doomed to live a wretched miserable life with no one to love, or to care for me? I shall wait anxiously for an answer, dear Addie. Will it be a favorable one?

My position in life, it is true, is not an elevated one, but I know and feel that I shall make a mark in life. God has given me talents and I shall improve them. I love you, Addie, and nothing else. Dare I hope that I am loved in return? Do not censure me, Addie, but remember that I have none to love or care for me. . . .

Hoping to soon receive an answer confirming my hopes.

I remain yours affectionately and forever

Charlie N. Tenney.

' The star-spangled banner in triumph shall wave,
O'er the land of the free and the home of the brave."

Addie sends a reply on January 26 which stresses that she loves Charlie as a sister loves a brother. However, her words imply that deeper feelings actually exist. Her language in this letter also illustrates her melodramatic nature. She speaks about how her heightened feelings for Charlie would bring shame upon her family. Clearly Addie was a virtuous woman of the 19th Century who had strong ideals about "proper behavior".

My brother,

How many, many happy thoughts have clustered round that substitute for Charlie. You, dear Charlie, would wish to dispel those thoughts – would you?

You may say I may hold in a happier nearer and dearer relation. But my friend the translation from a brother to a love is no common affair. I have taught my heart to love you only as a sister and have tried to have my love returned only as a brother. Charlie, I will confess that I could love you with the true and fervent passion of which my heart is capable, but Charlie the dark and dreadful disgrace resting upon our family!

I am sensible to the fact that there should be no blame attached to me. But darling brother you are too pure to unite yourself with one whom the world looks upon in such a light, or rather darkness, I may be too sensitive. I sometimes feel that I am, but my darling Charlie had I known of the facts I now do, I could never, never consented to correspond with you. I am thankful very thankful to Hallie for telling you. My heart and conscience often reproved me for not telling you myself, but I could not. My God! I would exclaim. I could not tell him if it even to save this nation! Was that a strong expression, my brother! My brother, what feelings arise upon the writing of that word when I know it is not sin? My darling I will not call you by that. I may by name, but as my own heart says, my own darling

Charlie which I feel to be true.

What am I writing, dear Charlie. Will you blush for Addie when you read these the sentiment of my heart? I fear you will, but Laurie [Addie's brother] was playing and singing one of my favorite pieces entitled "Heart Be Still" and it called out all the deeper feelings of my rebellious heart and seemed to work opposite from its usual course for my heart would not "be still" dear Charlie will you throw this from you in anger and say "she is nothing but a silly romantic school girl" Will you dear Charlie? If I knew you, I would not send it, but my darling, it is an ill tale but my hand has moved over if never before in unison with my heart and feelings.

Darling Charlie do you not think there is poetry on this page? I know there is in my heart but fie! What an expression I have written near the top of this page drawing the inference that the name of brother is cold. Bless me! Did I forget my own darling brother Hallie? No, a brother's name is not cold but a tumult of a different nature swept over me at that moment. Than fortune Laurie has stopped playing or I should again go off into one of my wild dreams that is my nature when I hear music, I either sit spell bound or else the inmost depth of my soul are awakened, but I must close this as Laurie wishing one to go to prayer meeting tonight with him.

May a guardian angel from Heaven hover round thee, forever as the earnest prayer of your

Addie

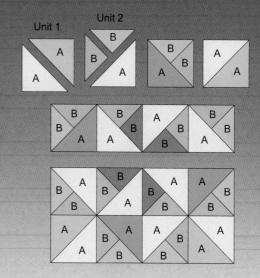

Windmill

Adelaide

6" finished

Fabrics required: Cream 4, Red 3, Green 2, Green 3 and Green 5

Cutting

From the Cream 4, cut:

✳ 6 – 2 3/8" squares. Cut each once on the diagonal to yield 12 A triangles.

From the Red 3, cut:

✳ 3 – 2 3/4" squares. Cut each on both diagonals to yield 12 B triangles.

From the Green 2, cut:

✳ 2 – 2 3/8" squares. Cut each once on the diagonal to yield 4 A triangles.

✳ 2 – 2 3/4" squares. Cut each on both diagonals to yield 8 B triangles.

From the Green 3, cut:

✳ 2 – 2 3/8" squares. Cut each once on the diagonal to yield 4 A triangles.

From the Green 5, cut:

✳ 1 – 2 3/4" squares. Cut each on both diagonals to yield 4 B triangles.

Piecing

Unit 1

✳ Half square triangle units

✳ Units are 1 1/2" finished.

✳ Sew a Cream 4 A triangle to a Green 2 A triangle. Press to the dark. Make 4.

Unit 2

✳ Units are 1 1/2" finished.

✳ Sew a Red 3 B triangle to a Green 2 B triangle along short side of triangles. Sew this unit to a Cream 4 A triangle to make a square. Make 4.

✳ Sew a Red 3 B triangle to a Green 2 B triangle along the short side of the triangles. Sew this unit to a Green 3 A triangle to make a square. Make 4.

✳ Sew a Red 3 B triangle to a Green 5 B triangle along the short side of the triangles Sew this unit to a Cream 4 A triangle to make a square. Make 4.

Block Assembly

Referring to the diagram lay out the pieced units in 4 rows. Sew the units together Sew the units together alternating the pressing direction with each row so your seams will nestle as you join your rows. Lay out the 4 rows and sew together.

Finishing the block

Refer to the instructions on page 66 and make the pieced setting for the Windmill block. The block will measure 25 1/2" finished.

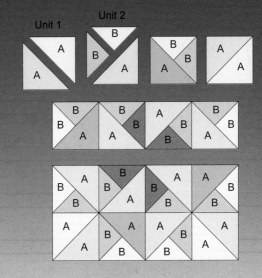

BLOCK 8
Windmill
Charlie

6" finished

Fabrics required: Cream 3, Cream 4, Blue 1, Brown 3 and Brown 2

Cutting

From the Cream 3, cut:

✳ 2 – 2 3/8" squares. Cut each once on the diagonal to yield 4 A triangles.

✳ 2 – 2 3/4" squares. Cut each on both diagonals to yield 8 B triangles.

From the Cream 4, cut:

✳ 6 - 2 3/8" squares. Cut each once on the diagonal to yield 12 A triangles.

From the Blue 1, cut:

✳ 3 – 2 3/4" squares. Cut each on both diagonals to yield 12 B triangles.

From the Brown 3, cut:

✳ 1 – 2 3/4" squares. Cut each on both diagonals to yield 4 Piece B triangles.

From the Brown 2, cut:

✳ 2 – 2 3/8" squares. Cut each once on the diagonal to yield 4 A triangles.

Piecing

Unit 1 – half square triangle units

✳ Units are 1 1/2" finished.

✳ Sew a Cream 4 A triangle to a Cream 3 A triangle. Press to the Cream 4. Make 4.

Unit 2

✳ Units are 1 1/2" finished.

✳ Sew a Blue 1 B triangle to a Cream 3 B triangle along short side of the triangles. Press to the blue. Sew this unit to a Cream 4 A triangle to make a square. Make 4.

✳ Sew a Blue 1 B triangle to a Cream 3 B triangle along the short side of the triangles. Press to the blue. Sew this unit to a Brown 2 A triangle to make a square. Make 4.

✳ Sew a Blue 1 B triangle to a Brown 3 B triangle along the short side of the triangles. Press to Brown 3. Sew this unit to a Cream 4 A triangle to make a square. Make 4.

Block Assembly

Referring to the diagram lay out the pieced units in 4 rows. Sew the units together Sew the units together alternating the pressing direction with each row so your seams will nestle as you join your rows. Lay out the 4 rows and sew together.

Finishing the block

Refer to the instructions on page 68 and make the pieced setting for the All Hallows block. The block will measure 18" finished.

CHAPTER 9

By **February** 4, Addie must have received Charles' many letters professing his love for her because she replies with a much more romantic and endearing letter:

Charlie My Darling,

Do you know how sweet those three word sound to me? And also how dear? No wonder I love to linger on these words but I must turn to other subjects. I must give you an account of my "days works." I have been engaged, (I think) in a good work today – not as noble a work as you are engaged in, but it is the best that I could do. I have been to the "Soldiers Aid Society" working real hard. . . ."

She writes several more letters over the next few days, each more excitedly expressing how she feels about Charlie. On February 9, she writes:

Darling, did you ever weep tears of joy? I know I did while reading your darling letter. Noble youth! How I thanked God, that there was one, not ashamed to own me as a friend.

Can you be happy in Addie's love? Then my own darling, be happy. For I confess, dear Charles, what to man I never before confessed – my love. A pure and fervent love – it is incessant as time itself. How long I have felt and known it I dare not own. For a time, I strove to clothe it in the appellations of "sister's regard" for you. A "sisterly interest" in your welfare. . . ."

Although the letter was not preserved, some correspondence from Charlie must have mentioned marriage. On February 11, Adelaide reveals her thoughts about marrying Charlie:

Dearest Charlie:

I had not cast a thought to avoid changing my name to the one you have at present. I had been so happy in your love that I had thought of nothing beyond. No Charlie, I must maintain the simple name of Addie De Case until I am something wiser, something better than I now am. I have aspirations that must be reached before I bear another name than this.

I wish to make myself worthy of you my darling, before I am wholly yours. And your love will strengthen me. Be content dearest at present, and remember that it is for the best for I could never bestow my hand upon you now. My heart is already yours and even will be, but my hand may not be for years. It may seem a hard request to grant when I ask you to not mention this again until I do, but you will grant it will you not my own Charlie! Does it seem a long time Charlie? Perhaps it does, but would you not rather wait a few years till I have a chance to cultivate the gifts God has given me than to find but too late that you have taken to your heart an unworthy object?

You asked me if father knew of our "carrying on" He does not. He always said that his daughters would never receive his dictation in choosing a companion. A queer person is my papa. He seems to think his children capable of choosing for themselves. Perhaps he is right. . . ."

Finally, on February 13, Adelaide mails Charlie her photograph. She had previously advised that she would not exchange pictures with a man that she did not intend to marry so this step was a solid signal to Charlie that her feelings were true.

Unaware that Adelaide's photograph is already on the way, Charlie composes a letter on February 15 asking her to send one.

My own darling Addie . . .

I know you are anxious to know every particular as regards my health, so I will say that with the exception of a very slight cold, I was never more healthy in my life.

. . . Have you any objection to trusting your miniature to my keeping now? In your letter of June 23d, you say, "I think that where a gentleman and lady are engaged, then they should change portraits." We are not really engaged, but may I not hope – nay, know that on the receipt of an answer to this that we are?

If you consent to change portraits, will you say yes? Mine! Be mine, love. I shall be so happy. This war cannot always last, and I can feel sure like living then. I am not rich Addie. I had been so happy that I scarcely bestowed a thought in that direction, and I fear I do wrong in asking you to become mine, poor as I am. Yet, I cannot help feeling that I am not wrong. Are you willing to accept me as I am, a soldier? Dependent upon myself? If you consent, I will strive to make you all that you wish.

Have you a spare picture for me, Addie, love?

From your loving

Charlie
who would die for you.

As Charlie's letter is making its way toward her, Adelaide has a horrible nightmare that is a harbinger of things to come. She writes him to describe what she dreamt on February 19:

"Oh! I had such a strange dream last night. I shudder even now when I think of it. You are lying ill and delirious where I could both see and hear you. You calling for me and yet I could not go to you. I struggled long earnestly and in vain, but there seemed some great obstacle between us which I could not surmount."

"Or any other man."   "That's what's the matter."

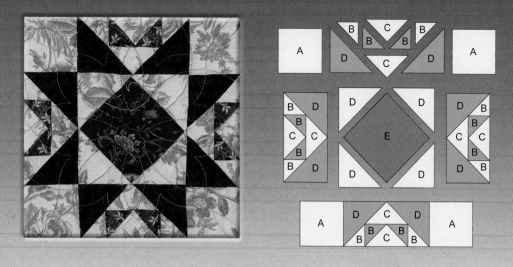

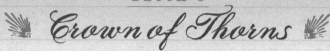

Crown of Thorns

Adelaide

6" finished

Fabrics required: Cream 1, Red 4, Green 2 and Green 3

Cutting

From the Cream 1, cut:

* 4 – 2" A squares.

* 4 – 1 5/8" squares. Cut each once on the diagonal to yield 8 B triangles.

* 2 – 2 3/4" squares. Cut each on both diagonals to yield 8 C triangles.

* 2 – 2 3/8" squares. Cut each once on the diagonal to yield 4 D triangles.

From the Red 4, cut:

* 4 – 2 3/8" squares. Cut each once on the diagonal to yield 8 D triangles.

From the Green 2, cut:

* 4 – 1 5/8" squares. Cut each once on the diagonal to yield 8 B triangles.

From the Green 3, cut:

* 1 – 2 5/8" E square.

Piecing

Square-in-a-square unit

* Unit is 3" finished.

* Sew 4 Cream 1 D triangles to the edges of the Green 3 E square. Press to the triangles. Make 1.

Star points units

* Units are 1 1/2" x 3" finished.

* Sew 2 Green 2 B triangles to each side of a Cream 1 C triangle. Sew 2 Cream 1 B triangles to each end of these units. Sew a Cream 1 C triangle to the top edge to form a large triangle. Last, sew a Red 4 D triangle to each short edge of this unit. Make 4.

Block Assembly

* Referring to the diagram lay out 2 A squares on either side of 1 star point unit. Sew together and press to the squares. Make 2.

* Lay out the 2 remaining star point units on either side of the square-in-a-square unit. Sew together and press to the square-in-a-square unit. Make 1.

* Lay out the 3 rows and sew together.

Finishing the block

Refer to the instructions on page 66 and make the pieced setting for the Crown of Thorns block. The block will measure 25 1/2" finished.

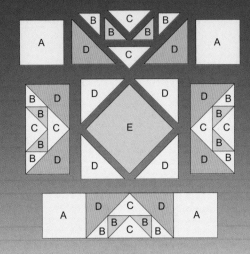

Crown of Thorns

Charlie

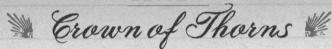

6" finished

Fabrics required: Cream 1, Blue 3 and Brown 1

Cutting

From the Cream 1, cut:

* 4 – 2" A squares.

* 4 – 1 5/8" squares. Cut each once on the diagonal to yield 8 B triangles.

* 2 – 2 3/4" squares. Cut each on both diagonals to yield 8 C triangles.

* 2 – 2 3/8" squares. Cut each once on the diagonal to yield 4 D triangles.

From the Blue 3, cut:

* 4 – 1 5/8" squares. Cut each once on the diagonal to yield 8 B triangles.

* 1 – 2 5/8" E square.

From the Brown 1, cut:

* 4 – 2 3/8" squares. Cut each once on the diagonal to yield 8 D triangles.

Piecing

Square-in-a-square unit

* Unit is 3" finished.

* Sew 4 Cream 1 D triangles to the edges of the Blue 3 E square. Press to the triangles. Make 1.

Star points units

* Units are 1 1/2" x 3" finished.

* Sew 2 Blue 3 B triangles to each side of a Cream 1 C triangle. Sew 2 Cream 1 B triangles to each end of these units. Sew a Cream 1 C triangle to the top edge to form a large triangle. Last, sew a Brown 1 D triangle to each short edge of this unit. Make 4.

Block Assembly

* Referring to the diagram lay out 2 A squares on either side of 1 star point unit. Sew together and press to the squares. Make 2.

* Lay out the 2 remaining star point units on either side of the square-in-a-square unit. Sew together and press to the square-in-a-square unit. Make 1.

* Lay out the 3 rows and sew together.

Finishing the block

Refer to the instructions on page 68 and make the pieced setting for the Crown of Thorns block. The block will measure 18" finished.

CHAPTER 10

While Charles' letter describing the incident was not preserved, Adelaide discovers that he was wounded in a battle at Kernstown, Va., on March 23, 1862.

Heaven reward you and bless you, my own my dear darling Charlie for your kind and precious letter of the 25th. Darling, you do not know how much it relieved my heart of an almost sinking fear and pain. Although it relieved me of my worst fears, yet it brought painful information that you did not escape unharmed.

Dearest, I know that you were injured far worse than you represented yourself to be. Do you not think that I could see in the very tone of your letter that it was with extreme pain that you could trace those dear lines? Oh, dear Charlie, please tell me just how badly your arm was hurt. Darling, why should you attempt to conceal from me your sufferings? Who should sooner know of your sufferings than one who has plighted her love, aye, even her life if necessary to you I could not feel worse dearest to know the entire truth than I now do. What, my Charlie trying to conceal from me – the one who should be with him through the hours of pain the extent of his wounds! Oh, do not my darling. The very thought is but frenzy. Why is it that I can not be with you? God only knows what I have suffered since I heard of that fearful battle. I had not heard from you for some time before that and when I read of the fight and still no word from Charlie. Then and only till then did I realize what life would be worth to me without you.

Oh, my darling. I am fearful that your wound is much more than you yourself think. But I must hope for the best. Is not this day beautiful? Oh the world is full of beauty when the heart is full of love, is it not. Charlie.

Write often very often to cheer the heart of your Addie

Over the next few months, Adelaide writes numerous letters describing her plans for a teaching career and seeking Charles' approval. His letters are slow to come and she grows increasingly worried about his safety. Finally, on August 13, Charlie writes to report about battles he has been in and casualties suffered by his regiment.

"I embrace the first opportunity I have to write you to appease you of my perfect safety. You have heard of the great battle of the 9th and must be anxious to learn of my fate. I escaped without a scratch, and am grateful to God for his mercy. I knew when I wrote you last that when an engagement should seem that we should be sent to the front. But I could not tell you, for I knew you would suffer so much on my account. Now that the battle is over, the rebels in full retreat and only 104 men left in the noble old 7th I can tell you. Gen. Pope said he wanted Tyler's Brigade (now Geary's) in the front "to set an example to the eastern troops" and nobly has the example been set. Our Regt went into the fight 290 strong, and came out with 104. . . ."

Charlie writes that the soldiers are frequently on the move and supplies like writing paper are hard to come by which explains his lack of correspondence. Then on August 18, Charlie writes the letter formally acknowledging that he has requested her hand in marriage:

My darling Addie,

While we were at Alexandria, I wrote a letter to your Papa, asking his consent to our union at any time you might specify, and I received a reply which made me very happy.

He says "If it is your and Addie's wish to connect your destinies for life, you shall have my best wishes and approval, unless that I shall learn of some dishonor attached to you, or her."

Ought I not to be happy, after receiving a reply like that? Do you wonder, my own, why I took such a course without informing you? I scarcely know myself, unless it was that I might have the pleasure of telling you myself, that he is not opposed to our union.

Have I your pardon, my Queen, for so palpable a wrong? Now that there is no obstacle intervening, there remains nothing but for you to denominate a day to consummate our union. I know my darling that it was your request that you should make the first allusion to this, but I feel an anxiety to know the time when you will be all mine. But of course there is the uncertainty of the time when I shall come home. . . .

My darling, I admire your patriotism but I could not say amen to your sacrificing your life, should I fall. Would it not be wrong? You know I enlisted to defend my country – with my life if needs be, and should I fall, and our country be saved, you should live and enjoy the fruit of our – of my labor. But I have passed through fires unharmed, while my comrades fell around me, and is not that all-powerful God able to still protect me – while you pray for me? He will do it."

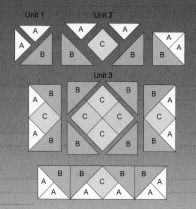

Salute to the Colors

Adelaide

6" finished

Fabrics required: Cream 2, Red 1, Red 3, Green 4 and Brown 1

Cutting

From the Cream 2, cut:

* 4 – 2 3/4" squares. Cut each on both diagonals to yield 16 A triangles.

From the Red 1, cut:

* 4 – 2 3/8" squares. Cut each once on the diagonal to yield 8 B triangles.

From the Red 3, cut:

* 2 – 1 1/2" C squares.

From the Green 4, cut:

* 6 – 1 1/2" C squares.

From the Brown 1, cut:

* 4 – 2 3/8" squares. Cut each once on the diagonal to yield 8 B triangles.

Piecing

Unit 1

* Units are 1 1/2" finished.

* Sew 2 Cream 2 A triangles together along the short side of the triangle. Press to one side. Sew a Red 1 B triangle to the long edge of the pieced triangle to make a square. Make 2.

* Sew 2 Cream 2 A triangles together along the short side of the triangle. Sew a Brown 1 B triangle to the long edge of the pieced triangle to make a square. Make 2.

Unit 2

* Units are 1 1/2" x 3" finished.

* Sew 2 Cream 2 A triangles to adjacent sides of a Green 4 C square. Press to the triangles. Sew a Brown 1 B triangle and a Red 1 B triangle to the short edges of the pieced unit. Make sure the color placement is correct. Press to the triangles. Make 4.

Unit 3

* Unit is 3" finished.

* Make a four-patch unit using 2 Green 4 C squares and 2 Red 3 C squares. Press to the dark. Make 1.

* Referring to the diagram for color placement, sew 2 Brown 1 B triangles to the opposite edges of the four-patch unit. Press to the triangles. Sew 2 Red 1 B triangles to the remaining edges of the four-patch unit. Press to the triangles.

Block Assembly

* Referring to the diagram lay out 2 Unit 1 squares on either side of a Unit 2 rectangle. Make sure the units are facing the correct direction. Sew together and press to the Unit 1 squares. Make 2.

* Lay out 2 Unit 2 rectangles on either side of the Unit 3 square. Make sure the units are facing the correct direction. Sew together and press to the Unit 3 square. Make 1.

* Lay out the 3 rows and sew together.

Finishing the block

Refer to the instructions on page 66 and make the pieced setting for the Salute to the Colors block. The block will measure 25 1/2" finished.

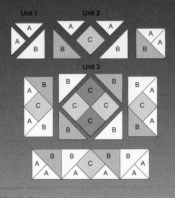

BLOCK 10

Salute to the Colors

Charlie

6" finished
Fabrics required: Cream 4, Blue 3, Blue 4, Blue 6, Brown 1 and Brown 2

Cutting

From the Cream 4, cut:

* 4 – 2 3/4" squares. Cut each on both diagonals to yield 16 A triangles.

From the Blue 3, cut:

* 4 – 1 1/2" C squares.

From the Blue 4, cut:

* 4 – 2 3/8" squares. Cut each once on the diagonal to yield 8 B triangles.

From the Blue 6, cut:

* 2 – 1 1/2" C squares.

From the Brown 1, cut:

* 4 – 2 3/8" squares. Cut each once on the diagonal to yield 8 B triangles.

From the Brown 2, cut:

* 2 – 1 1/2" C squares.

Piecing

Unit 1

* Units are 1 1/2" finished.

* Sew 2 Cream 4 A triangles together along the short side of the triangle. Press to one side. Sew a Blue 4 B triangle to the long edge of the pieced triangle to make a square. Make 2.

* Sew 2 Cream 4 A triangles together along the short side of the triangle. Sew a Brown 1 B triangle to the long edge of the pieced triangle to make a square. Make 2.

Unit 2

* Units are 1 1/2" x 3" finished.

* Sew 2 Cream 4 A triangles to adjacent sides of a Blue 3 C square. Press to the triangles. Sew a Brown 1 B triangle and a Blue 4 B triangle to the short edges of the pieced unit. Make sure the color placement is correct. Press to the triangles. Make 4.

Unit 3

* Unit is 3" finished.

* Make a four-patch unit using 2 Brown 2 C squares and 2 Blue 6 C squares. Press to the dark. Make 1.

* Referring to the diagram for color placement, sew 2 Brown 1 B triangles to the opposite edges of the four-patch unit. Press to the triangles. Sew 2 Blue 4 B triangles to the remaining edges of the four-patch unit. Press to the triangles.

Block Assembly

* Referring to the diagram lay out 2 Unit 1 squares on either side of a Unit 2 rectangle. Make sure the units are facing the correct direction. Sew together and press to the Unit 1 squares. Make 2.

* Lay out 2 Unit 2 rectangles on either side of the Unit 3 square. Make sure the units are facing the correct direction. Sew together and press to the Unit 3 square. Make 1.

* Lay out the 3 rows and sew together.

Finishing the block

Refer to the instructions on page 68 and make the pieced setting for the Salute to the Colors block. The block will measure 18" finished.

CHAPTER 11

Adelaide writes numerous letters to Charles throughout late summer and the early autumn of 1862. His replies are few and far between. In her letters, Addie describes her experiences as a new schoolteacher and daily life in her town. Occasionally, she reflects on the cost of war. Then, sometime in November, she learns that one reason she has not heard much from Charlie is that he has been ill. On November 11, Charlie wrote that he "had a slight attack of Liver Complaint. …" which had greatly weakened him. Upon learning of Charlie's illness, Addie wrote:

"When I read your letter darling – shall I tell you I wept? I did long very long. Not altogether a sorrowful weeping but partly joyful. Tears fell in sympathy for thee – best–beloved – that you should have suffered so much. Oh! how I thank you for unburdening your thoughts to me, darling Always let me share your sorrow as well as joy. How could parents act so indifferently about – but hush, Addie is not for you to censure – "God is just and every wrong shall die." Addie will not withhold the fervent "God bless thee my Charlie." Joyful tears flowed that I had ever made thee happy. God helping me you never shall regret loving Addie. And God will help me darling for I have asked him to. Are you so very happy dearest when you meditate upon my love? I have often wondered if ever mortal was so happy as I. But you seem to breathe my very thoughts.

I trust you have entirely recovered from your illness. It troubled me a good deal and I shall be very anxious to hear from you again. Pardon me dear but I feared you would not tell me just exactly how ill you were, I know it was a naughty thought but I could not help it. You will forgive me dear? . . . .

Love ever and now, your true

Addie

By late November, Adelaide learns that Charlie's illness has returned. She worries greatly about his condition in letter dated November 23, 1862:

My own loved Charlie,

How very much I thank you for your darling letter that arrived last evening. You know not, dearest how long and anxiously I had looked for a letter since you wrote of your recent indisposition. How I had prayed God to watch over thee in sickness and in health. How I had mourned over the fate that has kept such a barrier of miles twixt thee and me, best beloved, until I was nearly ill. If you would spare me pain my love, write often.

True your excuses were sufficient and I forgive you. Indeed the joy of once again hearing from you – of once again reading your own dear loving thoughts addressed to me darling more than canceled all the pain I had suffered. And art thou now well now darling? Art thou suffering far away from me with no kind hand to alleviate the pain?

Look to God dearest. He can relieve and be with you. For much as I regret it, I cannot be with you – only in spirit and that – always. How very thankful I am darling that you are in the position you now occupy instead of performing the arduous duties of camp life and marching As Carrie said (our Carrie Kibbee) when I told her where you were. "Oh! Addie, aren't you so glad." And in the dear girl's joy she actually kissed me.

Oh darling, how I wish you to come home. Were you here I do believe you would regain health and strength much faster than you now do. I would devote myself so much to your happiness that you could not help but get well. Do you not think so dear?

Did you intend darling to bid me hope when you said if the thing were possible you would come home this winter? If so, that you know a thousand times how much I wish you to return. Why you cannot know. . . .

Be very careful of your health dearest, and write very soon to your own true

Addie

As the days pass, Addie's foreboding grows. She writes Charlie again on December 8, 1862, to express her increasing concern.

My dear darling Charlie,

What a cold winter evening is this, but not cold enough to drive away warm loving thoughts from the heart. But with those same loving thoughts of thee dear, some are strangely mingled sad ones. And for several days previous to this, those same sad thoughts those I am almost tempted to say unwelcome forebodings have lingered about my heart – at times coming in to feel so very depressed in spirit as to not care whether life or death were near and at other times the warm tears would gush forth in torrents, and still I would not know for what I wept. Is it owing the fact that I do not oftener hear from you dearest? I know of nothing else that could cause such feeling in my heart. I know I am an ungrateful child but then you know the heart will be human in spite of our efforts to make it appear different at times, Oh, darling how very much I desire to see you. How very many long months have passed since "last we met" and God only knows how many more will pass before we shall meet again...

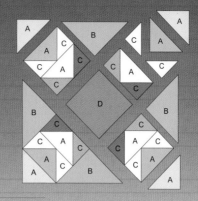

Wild Goose

Adelaide

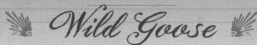

6" finished

Fabrics required: Cream 2, Cream 4, Red 1, Red 4, Red 5 and Green 1

Cutting

From the Cream 2, cut:

* 2 – 2 3/8" squares. Cut each once on the diagonal to yield 4 A triangles.
* 2 – 2 3/4" square. Cut on both diagonals to yield 8 C triangles.

From the Cream 4, cut:

* 2 – 2 3/8" squares. Cut each once on the diagonal to yield 4 A triangles.

From the Red 1, cut:

* 1 – 2 5/8" D square.

From the Red 4, cut:

* 1 – 2 3/4" square. Cut on both diagonals to yield 4 C triangles.

From the Red 5, cut:

* 1 – 2 3/4" square. Cut on both diagonals to yield 4 C triangles.

From the Green 1, cut:

* 2 – 2 3/8" squares. Cut each once on the diagonal to yield 4 A triangles.
* 1 – 4 1/4" square. Cut on both diagonals to yield 4 B triangles.

Piecing

Flying geese units

* Units are 1 1/2" x 2 1/2" finished
* Sew 2 Cream 2 C triangles to both sides of a Green 1 A triangle. Press to the triangles. Make 4.
* Referring to the diagram for color placement, sew a Red 5 C triangle to one side of a Cream 2 A triangle. Sew a Red 4 C triangle to the other side of the Cream 2 A triangle. Make 4.

Block assembly

Side sections

* Referring to the diagram for color placement, sew two flying geese units together. Sew a Green 1 B triangle to both sides of this flying geese unit. Press to the triangles. Sew a Cream 4 A triangle to the end of the unit. Press to the triangle. Make 2.

Middle section

* Referring to the diagram for color placement, sew two flying geese units together. Sew a Cream 4 A triangle to the end of this unit. Press to the triangle. Make 2.
* Sew 2 middle section units to either side of the Red 1 D square. Press to the square.
* Lay out the two side sections and middle section and sew together.

Finishing the block

* Refer to the instructions on page 66 and make the pieced setting for the Wild Goose block. The block will measure 25 1/2" finished.

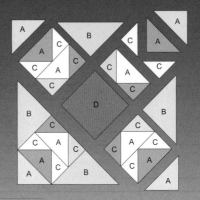

BLOCK 11

Charlie

6" finished

Fabrics required: Cream 1, Cream 6, Blue 3, Blue 4, Blue 6 and Brown 2

Cutting

From the Cream 1, cut:

✻ 2 – 2 3/8" squares. Cut each once on the diagonal to yield 4 A triangles.

From the Cream 6, cut:

✻ 2 – 2 3/8" squares. Cut each once on the diagonal to yield 4 A triangles.

✻ 2 – 2 3/4" square. Cut on both diagonals to yield 8 C triangles.

From the Blue 3, cut:

✻ 2 – 2 3/8" squares. Cut each once on the diagonal to yield 4 A triangles.

✻ 1 – 2 3/4" square. Cut on both diagonals to yield 4 C triangles.

From the Blue 4, cut:

✻ 1 – 4 1/4" square. Cut on both diagonals to yield 4 B triangles.

From the Blue 6, cut:

✻ 1 – 2 5/8" D square.

From the Brown 2, cut:

✻ 1 – 2 3/4" square. Cut on both diagonals to yield 4 C triangles.

Piecing

Flying geese units

✻ Units are 1 1/2" x 2 1/2" finished

✻ Sew 2 Cream 6 C triangles to both sides of a Blue 3 A triangle. Make 4.

✻ Referring to the diagram for color placement, sew a Brown 2 C triangle to one side of a Cream 6 A triangle. Sew a Blue 3 C triangle to the other side of the Cream 6 A triangle. Make 4.

Block assembly

Side sections

✻ Referring to the diagram for color placement, sew two flying geese units together. Sew a Blue 4 B triangle to both sides of this flying geese unit. Press to the triangles. Sew a Cream 1 A triangle to the end of the unit. Press to the triangle. Make 2.

Middle section

✻ Referring to the diagram for color placement, sew two flying geese units together. Sew a Cream 1 A triangle to the end of this unit. Press to the triangle. Make 2.

✻ Sew 2 middle section units to either side of the Blue 6 D square. Press to the square.

✻ Lay out the two side sections and middle section and sew together.

Finishing the block

Refer to the instructions on page 68 and make the pieced setting for the Wild Goose block. The block will measure 18" finished.

CHAPTER 12

As **Addie** worries, Charles' letter of November 25 is working its way toward her. He writes:

"My own loved Addie,

. . . Calm your fears my love, I am neither dead nor changed and I am enjoying better health than I have for three weeks past, and am steadily gaining, so that I think there is no immediate danger of my demise nor consignment to the Hospital. I must apologize for not writing within the past week as I promised to do. We have changed the Provost Marshal, and with the change came a great deal of work for "us four clerks," and we have had to keep hard at work from dawn of day until half past ten at night.

Darling – how much – oh! how much I wish to see you, to fold thee to my heart and gaze into those loving eyes – the windows of thy noble soul – to hear thy gentle voice as in accents full of love and tenderness, thou sayest, I love you.

But the splash of the rain falls upon my ear and I am "far away." The pleasure is denied me and I still toil on – a soldier in the good cause.

Addie – what would you say if I were to accept a discharge from the Army, and should come home? Would you say yes, or would you prefer that I should remain in the "Noble 7th" until it comes home to Cleveland with the "honors of war" . . .

Good night love, pleasant dreams be thine, and happiness. Write soon to your own loving and true

Charley

In December, though, Charlie's health again took a turn for the worse. She writes on December 10, urging Charlie to seek a discharge from the Army feeling they have both suffered enough:

Were I a true woman I expect I should tell you to remain if possible and defend our country. But love, I cannot. The sacrifice is too great. Our separation has been so long and such constant fear and anxiety has been borne so very long I feel as if we both need rest. Will you wonder what has become of my patriotism? It is all here yet. But I feel as if you had done your duty faithfully just as I desired you to do it.

Adelaide's letter of December 28 reveals she has received letters from Charles dated December 15, 18 and 19, however, those letters were not preserved.

Addie writes to Charles on January 7, 1863, begging him to send her news of his health. Then, on January 15, she writes again disclosing that she has received news from others that Charlie has relapsed and is not doing well:

Nothing could have give one greater pain then to know that you dearest, had suffered a relapse. Your last letter was so hopeful and charming that I was much encouraged, but as you my dearest "There is many a strife twixt the [illegible] and the life." May God in his great mercy give you strength so that you may not again be brought to your bed. I think there was nothing which kept me from utter despair, except the knowledge that you had received a furlough and that God willing, you will soon be home. But love, will not the exertion be too great? Will not the journey be too long for you to undertake in your weak state?

Oh Charlie, darling one I tremble. Would that you were but here, but I will be hopeful and trust in God's goodness...

How happy I should be love, could I but watch over you as you return to health, I do not believe anyone can do as well as I should. How devoted I should be. When the pain tortured you, I would try to drive it away and soothe you with gentle words, such as none but your Addie has a right to utter. Then when you were able and could endure it, I would read some splendid work, from which we could obtain instruction, and for one. Would be not be happy dearest?

In my dreams I was with you last night. I went to sleep wishing that I could fly to you. I had no sooner fallen into a gentle slumber than I was lifted from my bed and far, far away, over mountains, hills, rivers, cities and towns, on till at last I found myself in a dark comfortable room surrounded by [illegible]. Some were lying on rough beds, others walking around as if tired of life and wished to walk into eternity, I was told that I was in a hospital and that those frightful objects were dear brave soldiers.

Mentally, I asked if Charlie was there and began searching. Earnestly I gazed in each face hoping to see one familiar glance one loving one. I looked in one corner and noticed a rude couch of straw accompanied by my Charlie. I needed no second glance to convince me, besides over it born, his face animated and his blue-eyes humming with joy as he asked, "How are you?" I flew to thee darling. . . .

I remain as ever thine own true,

Addie

No other letters were preserved past January 15 so whether Charlie knew of Adelaide's concern as he grew more ill will never be known.

Charles Tenney died of dysentery on March 23, 1863 at Harper's Ferry.

Over the course of four years, more than 618,000 Americans died as a result of the war. The exact number is unknown due to poor record-keeping and the passage of time. Despite extensive research, we found no additional records about Adelaide Case following her last letters in 1863. How long did Addie wait before finally learning of Charlie's death? Upon hearing the news, what did she do? We can only wonder if Addie found love again or if she became a spinster. Whatever the outcome, Adelaide Case and Charles Tenney were able to carve out moments of happiness during a very unsettled time. Their legacy of finding hope and courage through their love lives on.

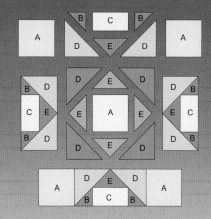

❧ Cross and Square ❧

Adelaide

6" finished

Fabrics required: Cream 1, Cream 4, Red 1, Red 3, Brown 1 and Green 4,

Cutting

From Cream 1, cut:

✳ 4 – 2" A squares.

From Cream 4, cut:

✳ 1 – 2" A square.

✳ 4 – 1 1/4" x 2" C rectangles.

From Red 1, cut:

✳ 2 – 2 3/8" squares. Cut each once on the diagonal to yield 4 D triangles.

From Red 3, cut:

✳ 1 – 2 3/4" square. Cut both diagonals to yield 4 E triangles.

From Green 4, cut:

✳ 4 – 2 3/8" squares. Cut each once on the diagonal to yield 8 D triangles.

From Brown 1, cut:

✳ 4 – 1 5/8" squares. Cut each once on the diagonal to yield 8 B triangles.

✳ 1 – 2 3/4" square. Cut both diagonals to yield 4 E triangles.

Piecing

Center square-in-a-square unit

✳ Unit is 3" square finished.

✳ Sew 4 Red 3 E triangles to the edges of a Cream 4 A square. Press to the triangles. Sew 4 Red 1 D triangles to the edges of this unit. Press to the triangles. Make 1.

Star points

✳ Units are 1 1/2" x 3" finished.

✳ Sew 2 Brown 1 B triangles to the sides of a Cream 4 C rectangle. Sew a Brown 1 E triangle to the top. Sew 2 D triangles to the sides. Make 4.

Block Assembly

✳ Referring to the diagram for placement lay out 2 Cream 1 A squares on either side of a star point unit. Make sure the star point unit is facing the correct direction. Sew together and press to the squares. Make 2.

✳ Lay out the 2 remaining star point units on either side of the center square-in-a-square unit. Sew together and press to the center unit. Make 1.

✳ Lay out the 3 rows and sew together.

Finishing the block

Refer to the instructions on page 66 and make the pieced setting for the Cross and Square block. The block will measure 25 1/2" finished.

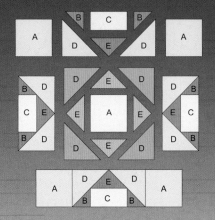

Cross and Square

Charlie

6" finished
Fabrics required: Cream 1, Cream 2, Blue 4, Blue 5, Brown 1 and Brown 2

Cutting

From Cream 1, cut:

* 4 – 2"A squares.

From Cream 2, cut:

* 1 – 2"A square.

* 4 – 1 1/4" x 2" C rectangles.

From Blue 4, cut:

* 4 – 2 3/8" squares. Cut each once on the diagonal to yield 8 D triangles.

From Blue 5, cut:

* 2 – 2 3/8" squares. Cut each once on the diagonal to yield 4 D triangles.

From Brown 1, cut:

* 4 – 1 5/8" squares. Cut each once on the diagonal to yield 8 B triangles.

* 1 – 2 3/4" square. Cut both diagonals to yield 4 E triangles.

From Brown 2, cut:

* 1 – 2 3/4" square. Cut both diagonals to yield 4 E triangles.

Piecing

Center square-in-a-square unit

* Unit is 3" square finished.

* Sew 4 Brown 2 E triangles to the edges of a Cream 2 A square. Press to the triangles. Sew 4 Blue 5 D triangles to the edges of this unit. Press to the triangles. Make 1.

Star points

* Units are 1 1/2" x 3" finished.

* Sew 2 Brown 1 B triangles to the sides of a Cream 2 C rectangle. Sew a Brown 1 E triangle to the top. Sew 2 Blue 4 D triangles to the sides. Make 4.

Block Assembly

* Referring to the diagram for placement lay out 2 Cream 1 A squares on either side of a star point unit. Make sure the star point unit is facing the correct direction. Sew together and press to the squares. Make 2.

* Lay out the 2 remaining star point units on either side of the center square-in-a-square unit. Sew together and press to the center unit. Make 1.

* Lay out the 3 rows and sew together.

Finishing the block

Refer to the instructions on page 68 and make the pieced setting for the Cross and Square block. The block will measure 18" finished.

Embroidery Instructions

Embroidered block and sashing for Charlie

* 18" finished
* To finish the Charlie quilt, you will need to embroider 6 blocks. If you prefer, you can substitute 6 – 18 1/2" plain setting blocks for the embroidered blocks.
* Fabric required: aged canvas (or muslin) and Blue 2
* Additional supplies: blue embroidery floss and needle

From the aged canvas, cut:

* 1 – 15" square.

Enlarge the embroidery pattern (found on pages 60-65) 200%. Fold the aged canvas square in half and half again to use as registration marks. Lightly trace the pattern onto the aged canvas. Embroider using three strands of floss. Once the embroidery is finished, trim the block to 14 1/2" square.

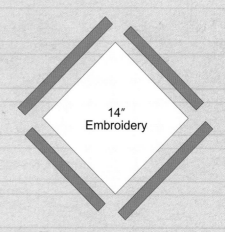

14"
Embroidery

From the Blue 2, cut:

* 2 – 2 1/2" x 14 1/2" strips.
* 2 – 2 1/2" x 18 1/2" strips.

Referring to the diagram, sew 2 – 14 1/2" strips to either side of the embroidered block. Press to the strips. Repeat with the remaining 2 strips.

I love you
with a pure, fervent
affection which comes
welling up from
my heart

How many
noble sentiments are
cherished in the heart
which are never
brought to light.

"If happiness exists among soldiers, it is him who feels that her spirit is watching over him"

"I love you with a pure, feruent affection which comes welling up from my heart."

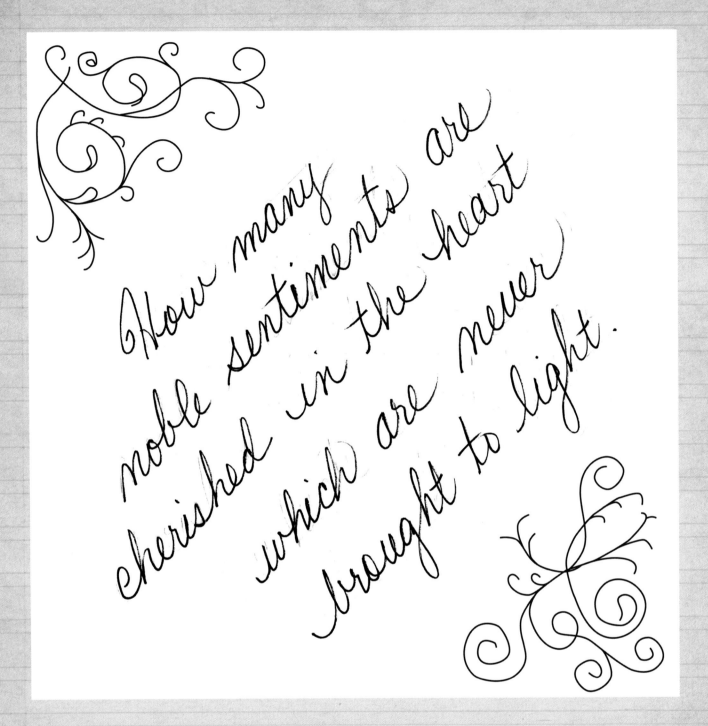

"How many noble sentiments are cherished in the heart which are never brought to light"

"Mine! be mine, love. I shall so be happy."

"Always let me share your sorrow as well as joy."

"My love, a pure and feruent love, it is incessant as time itself."

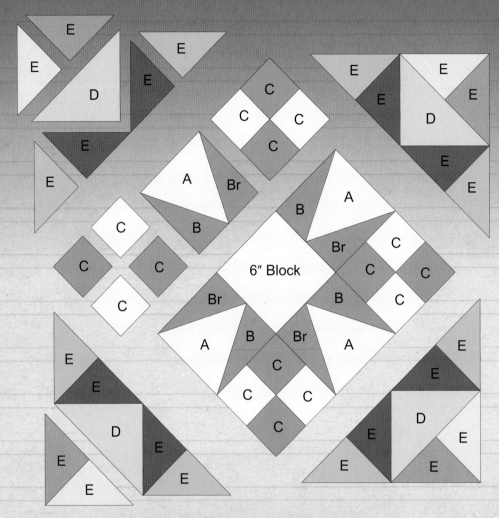

Pieced setting for Adelaide

Once your 12 – 6" blocks are finished, you'll need to add a pieced setting to make it finish at 25 1/2".

Fabrics required: Cream 1, Cream 3, Red 1, Red 5, Red 4, Green 1 and Green 4

From Cream 1, cut:
* 8 – 3 1/2" C squares.
* 4 – Template A triangles.
* 2 – 7 1/4" squares. Cut in half on the diagonal to form 4 D triangles.

From Cream 3, cut:
* 1 – 7 5/8" square. Cut in half on **both** diagonals to form 4 E triangles.

From Red 1, cut:
* 4 – Template B triangles
* 4 – Template Br triangles.

From Red 4, cut:
* 2 – 7 5/8" squares. Cut in half on **both** diagonals to form 8 E triangles.

From Red 5, cut:
* 1 – 7 5/8" square. Cut in half on **both** diagonals to form 4 E triangles.

From Green 1, cut:
* 8 – 3 1/2" C squares.

From Green 4, cut:
* 2 – 7 5/8" squares. Cut in half on **both** diagonals to form 8 E triangles.

Star Block

Four-patch units
* Units are 6" finished.
* Make a four-patch unit using 2 Green 1 C squares and 2 Cream 1 C squares. Press to the dark. Make 4.

Star points
* Units are 6" finished
* Sew a Red 1 B and Br triangle to either side of a Cream 1 A triangle. Press to the red. Make 4.
* Referring to the diagram for placement, sew 2 four-patch units to either side of 1 star point unit. Press to the four-patches. Make 2.
* Sew the remaining two star point units to either side of the 6" block. Press to the block. Make 1.
* Sew the three rows together to create an 18" finished star block.

Corner Units
* For the corner units used to set the 18" star block on point, piece as follows.

Triangle units
* Sew a Cream 3 E triangle to a Red 5 E triangle along the short edge. Press to the dark. Make 4.

Flying geese units
* Sew 2 Red 4 E triangles to either side of the Cream 1 D triangle. Press to the red. Make 4.
* Sew a Green 4 E triangle to each end of the flying geese unit. Press to the triangles. Make 4.
* Referring to the diagram for placement, sew a triangle unit to the top of the flying geese unit. Press to the triangle units. Make 4.
* Sew the 4 corner units to each side of the star block to create a 25 1/2" finished block.

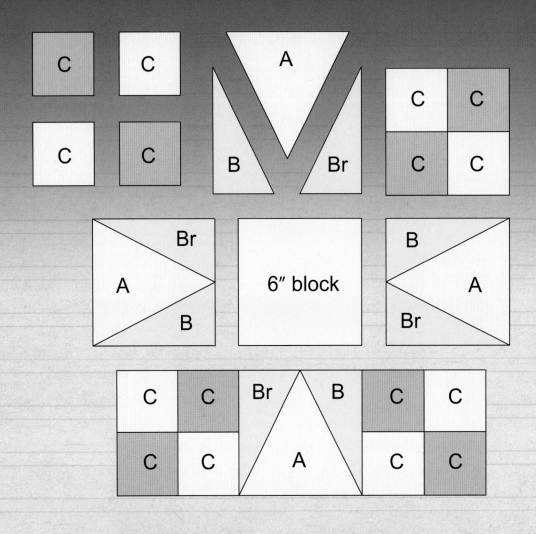

Pieced setting for Charlie

Once your 12 – 6" blocks are finished, you'll need to add a pieced setting to make it finish at 18".

Fabrics required: Cream 6, Blue 4 and Brown 1

From Brown 1, cut:

* ✳ 8 – 3 1/2" C squares.

From Cream 6, cut:

* ✳ 8 – 3 1/2" C squares.
* ✳ 4 – Template A triangles.

From Blue 4, cut:

* ✳ 4 – Template B triangles
* ✳ 4 – Template Br triangles.

Star Block

* ✳ Four-patch units
* ✳ Units are 6" finished.
* ✳ Make a four-patch unit using 2 Brown 1 C squares and 2 Cream 6 C squares. Press to the dark. Make 4.

Star points

* ✳ Units are 6" finished
* ✳ Sew a Blue 4 B and Br triangle to either side of a Cream 6 A triangle. Press to the blue. Make 4.
* ✳ Referring to the diagram for placement, sew 2 four-patch units to either side of 1 star point unit. Press to the four-patches. Make 2.
* ✳ Sew the remaining two star point units to either side of the 6" block. Press to the block. Make 1.
* ✳ Sew the three rows together to create an 18" finished star block.

Finishing for Adelaide

93 ½" X 119"

Quilt top center

Referring to the assembly diagram, sew the 12 blocks together in 4 rows of 3 blocks each. The top center should measure 76 1/2" x 102" finished.

Borders

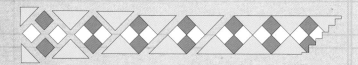

Fabrics required: Red 5, Red 6 and Cream 2

From the Red 5, cut:
* 92 – 3 1/2" squares.

From the Cream 2, cut:
* 92 – 3 1/2" squares.

From the Red 6, cut:
* 21 – 9 3/4" squares. Cut on **both** diagonals to yield 84 triangles
* 8 – 5 1/8" squares. Cut each once on the diagonal to yield 16 triangles.

Four-patch units
* Units are 6" finished.
* Make a four-patch unit using 2 Red 5 squares and 2 Cream 2 squares. Press to the dark. Make 46.

Side borders
* Lay out 12 four-patch units, 22 large triangles and 4 small triangles. Referring to the diagram, assemble the triangles and four-patch blocks in a row. Press to the triangles. Make 2.

Top and bottom borders
* Lay out 11 four-patch units, 20 large triangles and 4 small triangles. Referring to the diagram, assemble the triangles and four-patch blocks in a row. Press to the triangles. Make 2.

Quilt top assembly
* Sew the side borders to the quilt. Press to the borders. Sew the top and bottom borders to the quilt. Press to the borders.

Binding

From the Red 7, cut:
* 11 – 2 1/2" x width of fabric strips.
* Piece together strips to create about 440" of binding. Bind quilt after quilting.

Finishing for Charlie

93 1/2" X 119"

To finish the quilt, you will need to cut 10 Cream 1 side setting triangles and 4 Cream 1 corner setting triangles to join with the 12 pieced blocks and 6 embroidered blocks.

Quilt top center

From the Cream 1, cut:

* 3 – 26 5/8" squares. Cut each on both diagonals to yield 12 triangles to be used as side setting triangles. You will only use 10 in the piecing.

* 2 – 13 5/8" squares and cut once diagonally to make 4 corner setting triangles.

* Referring to the assembly diagram, lay out the pieced blocks, embroidered blocks and setting triangles. Sew together in diagonal rows. Join the rows to create the top center. The top should measure 76 1/2" x 102" finished.

Borders

Fabrics required: Blue 6, Blue 7, Cream 5

From the Blue 6, cut:
* 92 – 3 1/2" squares.

From the Cream 5, cut:
* 92 – 3 1/2" squares.

From the Blue 7, cut:
* 21 – 9 3/4" squares. Cut on both diagonals to yield 84 triangles

* 8 – 5 1/8" squares. Cut each once on the diagonal to yield 16 triangles.

Four-patch units
* Units are 6" finished.

* Make a four-patch unit using 2 Blue 6 squares and 2 Cream 5 squares. Press to the dark. Make 46.

Side borders
* Lay out 12 four-patch units, 22 large triangles and 4 small triangles. Referring to the diagram, assemble the triangles and four-patch blocks in a row. Press to the triangles. Make 2.

Top and bottom borders
* Lay out 11 four-patch units, 20 large triangles and 4 small triangles. Referring to the diagram, assemble the triangles and four-patch blocks in a row. Press to the triangles. Make 2.

Quilt top assembly
* Sew the side borders to the quilt. Press to the borders. Sew the top and bottom borders to the quilt. Press to the borders.

Binding

From the Blue 8, cut:
* 11 – 2 1/2" x width of fabric strips.

* Piece together strips to create about 440" of binding. Bind quilt after quilting.

Rocky Mountain Stars

Rocky Mountain Stars

DESIGNED AND MADE BY DOLORES SMITH AND SARAH MAXWELL

QUILT SIZE: 83" X 100"
BLOCKS FINISH: 12" SQUARE

When a beautiful background print was available in three different colorways, we decided to use all three to add subtle interest to the quilt.

Fabrics

* 3/4 yard of light blue print for background 1 for blocks
* 1 yard of light brown floral print for background 2 for blocks
* 1 yard of light green floral print for background 3 for blocks
* 12-16 fat quarters of assorted medium to dark prints in shades of green, blue, double pink, red, gold and cheddar for blocks
* 1 yard of dark brown 1 for blocks and setting triangles
* 1 yard of medium green for blocks and setting triangles
* 1 2/3 yards of golden tan for setting triangles
* 2/3 yard of beige print for inner border
* 2 yards of orange print for outer border
* 1 yard of dark brown 2 for binding

CUTTING – BLOCK 1

Block 1 Diagram

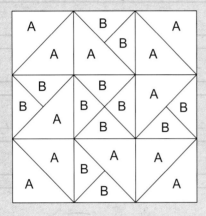

Cutting Diagram

Make 8

The 8 blocks on the top and bottom rows all have the same corner colors with different colors in the centers.

To construct one of these blocks, you will need background 1, dark brown 1, the medium green and 3 different colored prints per block. Use a different color combination for the 3 colored prints for each of the remaining 7 blocks, but the corners and background stay the same in all 8.

From background 1, cut:

* 2 – 4 7/8" squares. Cut in half on the diagonal to form 4 A triangles.

* 1 – 5 1/4" square. Cut in half on **both** diagonals to form 4 B triangles.

From dark brown 1, cut:

* 2 – 4 7/8" squares. Cut in half on the diagonal to form 4 A triangles. (You will only use 3 in the piecing).

From the medium green, cut:

* 1 – 4 7/8" square. Cut in half on the diagonal to form 2 A triangles. (You will only use 1 in the piecing).

From 1 colored print, cut:

* 1 – 5 1/4" square and cut in half on **both** diagonals to form 4 B triangles. (You will only use 2 in the piecing).

From a different colored print, cut:

* 2 – 5 1/4" squares. Cut in half on **both** diagonals to form 8 B triangles. (You will only use 6 in the piecing).

From a third colored print, cut:

* 2 – 4 7/8" squares and cut in half on the diagonal to form 4 A triangles. (These are the large star points.)

Piecing

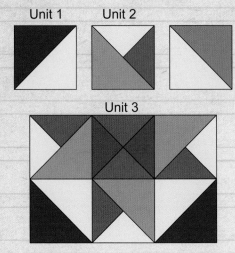

Unit 1   Unit 2

Unit 3

Piecing Diagram

Unit 1

✳ Sew 3 background A triangles to 3 dark brown A triangles to form 3 half-square triangle units. Press to the brown. Sew 1 background A triangle to 1 medium green A triangle to form 1 half-square triangle unit. Press to the green.

Unit 2

✳ Sew a colored print B triangle to a background B triangle along short side of triangles. Press to the dark. Sew this unit to a colored print (large star point) A triangle to make a square. Press to the colored print. Make 4.

Unit 3

✳ Sew 2 colored print B triangles to the remaining 2 colored print B triangles along short side of triangles. Sew these units together to make a square.

Referring to the Block 1 Diagram lay out the pieced units in 3 rows. Sew the units together alternating the pressing direction with each row so your seams will nestle as you join your rows. Lay out the 3 rows and sew together.

Repeat to make 7 more blocks, changing the center fabrics.

Block 2 Diagram

Make 12

Block 2 is cut and pieced just as you did Block 1, only the color placement on the corners and the background has changed.

To construct one of these blocks, you will need background 2, dark brown 1, the medium green and 3 different colored prints per block. Use a different color combination for the 3 colored prints for each of the remaining 11 blocks, but the corners and background stay the same in all 12.

From dark brown 1, cut:

✳ 1 – 4 7/8" squares. Cut in half on the diagonal to form 2 A triangles.

From background 2, cut:

✳ 2 – 4 7/8" squares. Cut in half on the diagonal to form 4 A triangles.

✳ 1 – 5 1/4" square. Cut in half on **both** diagonals to form 4 B triangles.

From the medium green, cut:

✳ 1 – 4 7/8" square. Cut in half on the diagonal to form 2 A triangles.

From 1 colored print, cut:

✳ 1 – 5 1/4" square and cut in half on **both** diagonals to form 4 B triangles. (You will only use 2 in the piecing).

From a different colored print, cut:

✳ 2 – 5 1/4" squares. Cut in half on **both** diagonals to form 8 B triangles. (You will only use 6 in the piecing).

From a third colored print, cut:

✳ 2 – 4 7/8" squares and cut in half on the diagonal to form 4 A triangles. (These are the large star points.)

Piece together using the same directions found in Block 1 making sure the corner units look like the Block 2 Diagram.

Repeat to make 11 more blocks, changing the center fabrics.

CUTTING – BLOCK 3

Block 3 Diagram

Make 12

Block 3 is cut and pieced just as you did Blocks 1 and 2, only the background has changed.

To construct one of these blocks, you will need background 3, dark brown 1, the medium green and 3 different colored prints per block. Use a different color combination for the 3 colored prints for each of the remaining 11 blocks, but the corners and background stay the same in all 12.

From dark brown 1, cut:

✳ 1 – 4 7/8" squares. Cut in half on the diagonal to form 2 A triangles.

From background 3, cut:

✳ 2 – 4 7/8" squares. Cut in half on the diagonal to form 4 A triangles.

✳ 1 – 5 1/4" square. Cut in half on **both** diagonals to form 4 B triangles.

From the medium green, cut:

✳ 1 – 4 7/8" square. Cut in half on the diagonal to form 2 A triangles.

From 1 colored print, cut:

✳ 1 – 5 1/4" square and cut in half on **both** diagonals to form 4 B triangles. (You will only use 2 in the piecing).

From a different colored print, cut:

✳ 2 – 5 1/4" squares. Cut in half on **both** diagonals to form 8 B triangles. (You will only use 6 in the piecing).

From a third colored print, cut:

✳ 2 – 4 7/8" squares and cut in half on the diagonal to form 4 A triangles. (These are the large star points.)

✳ Piece together using the same directions found in Block 1 making sure the corner units look like the Block 3 Diagram.

Repeat to make 11 more blocks, changing the center fabrics.

Setting and corner triangles

The setting triangles are made of the golden tan print with a print traingle to continue the design of the quilt. Six setting triangles use the medium green print, 8 use the dark brown print.

Cutting

For the setting triangles:

From medium green print, cut:

* 3 – 4 7/8” squares. Cut in half on the diagonal to form 6 triangles.

From Dark Brown 1, cut:

* 4 – 4 7/8” squares. Cut in half on the diagonal to form 8 triangles.

From the golden tan print, cut:

* 14 – 6 1/8” x 18 1/4” strips. Use the 45º markings on your ruler to cut both ends of the strip to form a trapezoid as shown in the diagram.

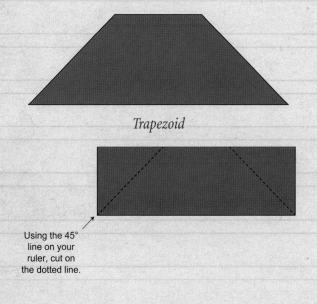

Trapezoid

Using the 45°
line on your
ruler, cut on
the dotted line.

Cutting for Trapezoid

Sew a medium green triangle to the short side of 6 **trapezoids.** Sew a dark brown triangle on the short side of 8 **trapezoids** as shown in the Setting Triangle diagrams.

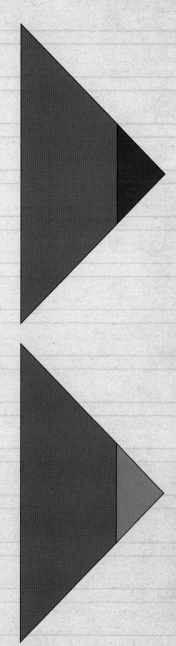

Green Setting Triangle and Brown Setting Triangle

For the corner triangles:

From the golden tan print, cut:

* 2 – 9 3/8” squares. Cut in half on the diagonal to form 4 triangles.

Putting it all together

Lay out the blocks as shown in the Quilt Assembly Diagram, with the blue background blocks on the top and bottom row. Alternate the green and brown background blocks in the center of the quilt. The quilt is sewn together in diagonal rows.

Borders

Inner border

From the **beige print**, cut 9 – 2" wide strips x width of fabric.

✳   Measure the length of your quilt top. Piece together the beige strips to equal the length. Sew the strips to the sides of the quilt top and press to the border.

✳   Now, measure the width of your quilt. Piece together the beige strips to equal the width. Sew the strips to the sides of the quilt top and press to the border.

Outer border

From the **orange print**, cut 10 – 6 1/2" wide strips x width of fabric.

✳   Measure the length of your quilt top. Piece together the orange strips to equal the length. Sew the strips to the sides of the quilt top and press to the border.

✳   Now, measure the width of your quilt. Piece together the orange strips to equal the width. Sew the strips to the sides of the quilt top and press to the border.

Finishing

Quilt as desired and bind with dark brown 2.

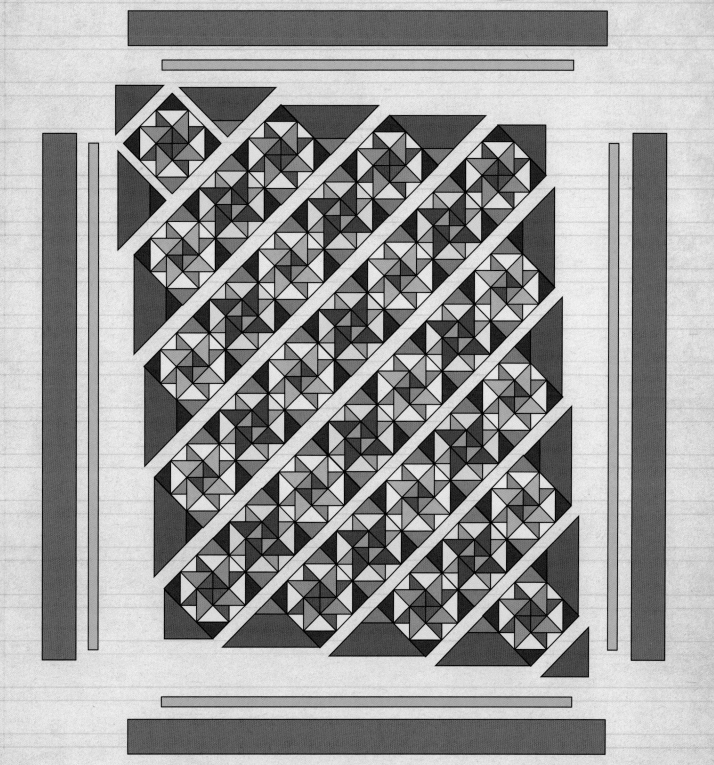

Quilt Assembly Diagram

Crossing Paths

Crossing Paths

DESIGNED AND MADE BY DOLORES SMITH AND SARAH MAXWELL

QUILT SIZE: 80" SQUARE
BLOCKS FINISH: 10" SQUARE

When our shop was featured in Quilt Sampler, Fall 2007, one of the pictured quilts was a project called Crossing Paths. The quilt was designed to use lots and lots of 1800s prints while still having a coordinated look. Crossing Paths is now available to all who have asked for directions on how to make it over the years. Select your favorite 1800s prints following the guidelines below and enjoy.

Fabrics

✶ Fat quarters of 16 different blue prints ranging from medium blue to navy

✶ Fat quarters of 16 different light background prints

✶ Fat eighths (9" x 22") of 24 prints in assorted colors. Look for shades of green, brown, red and purple as the additional colors.

✶ 3/4 yard of a blue print for binding

The quilt is composed of 64 – 10" blocks set 8 rows across and 8 rows down.

Cutting

Cutting Diagram

To make one block cut as follows:

From the background print, cut:

✶ 6 – 2 1/2" A squares.

✶ 4 – 2 7/8" squares. Cut each in half on the diagonal to make 8 B triangles.

From the blue print, cut:

✶ 6 – 2 1/2" A squares.

✶ 4 – 2 7/8" squares. Cut each in half on the diagonal to make 8 B triangles.

From the colored print, cut:

✶ 5 – 2 1/2" A squares.

Row 1:

Row 2:

Row 3:

Row 4:

Row 5:

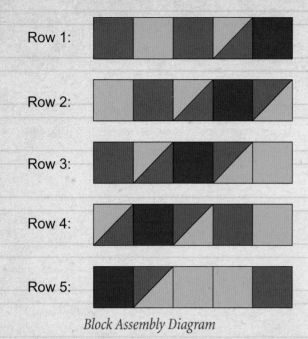

Block Assembly Diagram

Refer to the diagram for placement. **Note: As a general rule, press seams to the darker fabric, for Crossing Paths, that means the seams are generally pressed to the blue prints.**

✳ Sew a B background triangle to a B blue triangle to form a half-square triangle unit. Make 8.

✳ Lay out the block according to the diagram and piece together, row by row. Rows 2 and 4 are assembled in the same order and just rotated when the block is assembled.

✳ Repeat these steps to make 63 additional blocks.

Putting It All Together:

✳ Referring to the quilt assembly diagram, rotate the blocks to form the diagonal chain pattern shown. The blocks are set together with 8 blocks in each row and 8 total rows. Pay careful attention to the rotation of the blocks.

✳ Quilt as desired and bind with the blue print.

Quilt Assembly Diagram

Blue Ridge Baskets

Blue Ridge Baskets

DESIGNED AND MADE BY DOLORES SMITH AND SARAH MAXWELL

QUILT SIZE: 62" X 79"

BLOCKS FINISH: 12" SQUARE

The small-scale background prints on white joined with the varying shades of blue prints combine for a quilt with classic appeal.

Fabrics

The quilt is composed of 18 different basket blocks. There are 17 different blue prints in the Bonnie's Blues line. We used each blue once and repeated the dark blue from the outer border in a second block for a total of 18 blocks. There are 7 different background prints in the line. We used each twice and then used the fabric left from the one yard cuts of background prints for the last four blocks.

7 assorted background prints (5 1/3 yards total)

* 1 yard each of 2 fabrics

* 2/3 yards each of 5 fabrics

17 assorted blue prints (About 8 yards total)

* 2/3 yard medium blue for the inner border and 1 block

* 2 1/4 yards dark blue for the outer border, binding and 2 blocks

* Fat thirds (22" x 24") or 1/3 yard of 15 assorted medium and dark blue prints (4 7/8 yards total)

Cutting

Outer Border

From the dark blue print, cut:

* 4 – 4 1/2" x width of fabric strips. Piece together to form 2 – 62 1/2" long borders.

* 4 – 4 1/2" x width of fabric strips. Piece together to form 2 – 71 1/2" long borders.

Inner Border

From the medium blue print, cut:

* 3 – 2" x width of fabric strips. Piece together to form 2 – 54 1/2" long borders.

* 4 – 2" x width of fabric strips. Piece together to form 2 – 68 1/2" long borders.

Corner Triangles

From 2 background fabrics, cut:

* 1 – 9 3/8" squares. Cut in half on the diagonal to yield 4.

Side Setting Triangles

From 3 background fabrics, cut:

* 1 – 18 1/4" square. Cut in half on **both** diagonals to yield 4 triangles from each print. You will use 10 of these triangles along the outer edges of the quilt. Two may be discarded.

Binding

From the dark blue print, cut:

* 8 – 2 1/2" x width of the fabric strips for double-fold binding.

Blocks

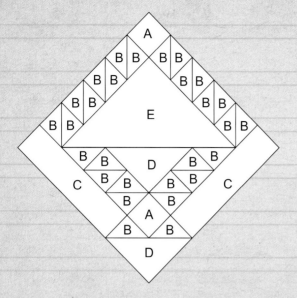

To make one block cut as follows:

From the background print, cut:

* 2 – 2 1/2" A squares.

* 6 – 2 7/8" squares. Cut in half on the diagonal to make 12 B triangles.

* 2 – 2 1/2" x 8 1/2" C rectangles.

* 1 – 4 7/8" square. Cut in half on the diagonal to make 2 D triangles. Use 1 D triangle in this block. Save the extra triangle for a second block

* 1 – 8 7/8" square. Cut in half on the diagonal to make 2 E triangles. Use 1 E triangle in this block. Save the extra triangle for a second block

From the blue print, cut:

* 8 – 2 7/8" squares. Cut in half on the diagonal to make 16 B triangles.

* 1 – 4 7/8" square. Cut in half on the diagonal to make 2 D triangles. Use 1 D triangle in this block. Save the extra triangle for a second block

Piecing

Block Assembly Diagram

* Refer to the diagram for placement. **Note:** As a general rule, press seams to the darker fabric.

* Sew a background B triangle to a blue B triangle to form a half-square triangle unit. Make 12.

* Sew 2 half-square triangle units together and then add a blue B triangle to the top edge as shown. Repeat with a second set of half-square triangle units and a blue triangle making sure to angle the blue triangle in the opposite direction.

* Sew a background A square to the end of one of these units. Sew the other unit to the short side of a blue D triangle. Sew these two units together referring to the diagram above.

* Sew the background E triangle to this pieced triangle unit.

* Sew the remaining 8 half-square triangle units into 2 rows as shown. Add a background A square to the end of one row. Sew the short row of half-square triangle units onto the left side of the E background triangle and then the long row of half-square triangle units and square onto the right side of the E background triangle, referring to the diagram above and paying careful attention to placement.

* Sew a blue B triangle to the end of a background C rectangle. Repeat with the remaining triangle and

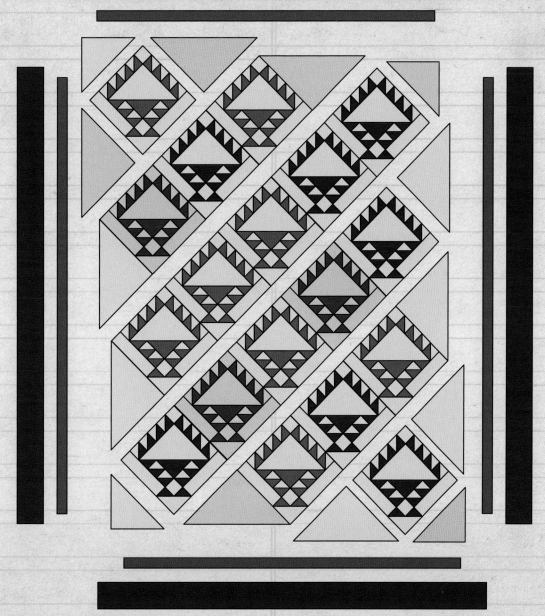

Quilt Assembly Diagram

rectangle referring to the diagram for how to position the triangles.

✳ Sew these pieced strips around the pieced center unit.

✳ Sew the background D triangle to the bottom of the block. Your block should measure 12 1/2" unfinished. Make 18.

Putting It All Together

This quilt is assembled in diagonal rows. Referring to the quilt assembly diagram, assemble the rows, adding a corner triangle to each of the 4 corners and adding side triangles to the ends of the rows. Continue assembling the rows until the interior of the quilt is sewn together.

Attach the inner medium blue and outer dark blue borders to the quilt. We typically sew the longest border on first, so in this case we would sew the side borders on first, then the top and bottom borders. Press to the borders.

Quilt as desired and bind with the dark blue print.

Autumn Ties

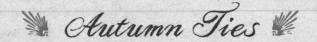

Autumn Ties

DESIGNED AND MADE BY DOLORES SMITH AND SARAH MAXWELL

QUILT SIZE: 60" X 72"

BLOCKS FINISH: 12" SQUARE

The simple Bowtie block subtly shines when paired with vintage fabrics in an autumn palette.

Fabrics

* ✳ 7/8 yard **each** of two different light tonal prints for backgrounds
* ✳ 2 1/4 – 2 1/2 yards total of assorted medium to dark prints
* ✳ 1/2 yard of a stripe for inner border
* ✳ 1 1/4 yards of a floral for outer border
* ✳ 2/3 yard of dark print for binding

The quilt is composed of 20 – 12" blocks set 4 blocks across and 5 blocks down. Two borders frame the blocks to finish the quilt.

Cutting

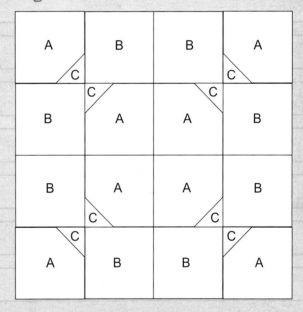

Cutting Diagram

From background print 1, cut:
* ✳ 4 – 3 1/2" A squares.

From background print 2, cut:
* ✳ 4 – 3 1/2" A squares.

From each of 4 different medium to dark prints, cut:
* ✳ 2 – 3 1/2" B squares.
* ✳ 2 – 2 1/8" squares. (Will become C triangles.)

Piecing

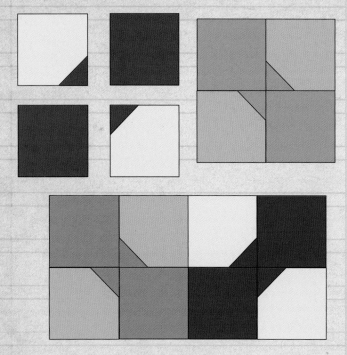

Block Assembly

* Refer to the diagram for placement. **Note: As a general rule, press seams to the darker fabric.**

* Press 1 – 2 1/8" square in half on the diagonal. Open and place on the corner of 1 background square. Sew the small square to the large sqauare using the pressed line as a guide. Press small triangle open to make 1 large square. Make 8 – 2 of each color.

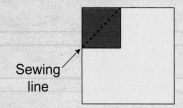

Sewing line

* Lay out 2 matching B squares and 2 matching background squares. Sew together as a four-patch block, pressing to the dark. Repeat with remaining 3 colors. Lay out the 4 units and sew together as shown in the Assembly Block Diagram. Make 20.

Putting It All Together

* Referring to the Quilt Assembly Diagram, lay out out the blocks as shown. The blocks are set together with 4 blocks in each row and 5 total rows.

* From the inner border fabric, cut 1 3/4" strips from the striped fabric and piece together 2 strips measuring 1 3/4" x 51" and 2 strips measuring 1 3/4" x 60 1/2". Attach the strips to the sides of the quilt first. Press toward the stripe fabric. Then attach the borders to the top and bottom of the quilt.

* From the outer border fabric, cut 5" strips and piece together 2 strips measuring 5" x 63" and 2 strips measuring 5" x 60". Attach the strips to the sides of the quilt first. Press toward the striped fabric. Then attach the borders to the horizontal top and bottom of the quilt.

* Quilt as desired and bind with the dark print

Quilt Assembly Diagram

MARCUS Fabrics®

Adelaide Fabric by Faye Burgos

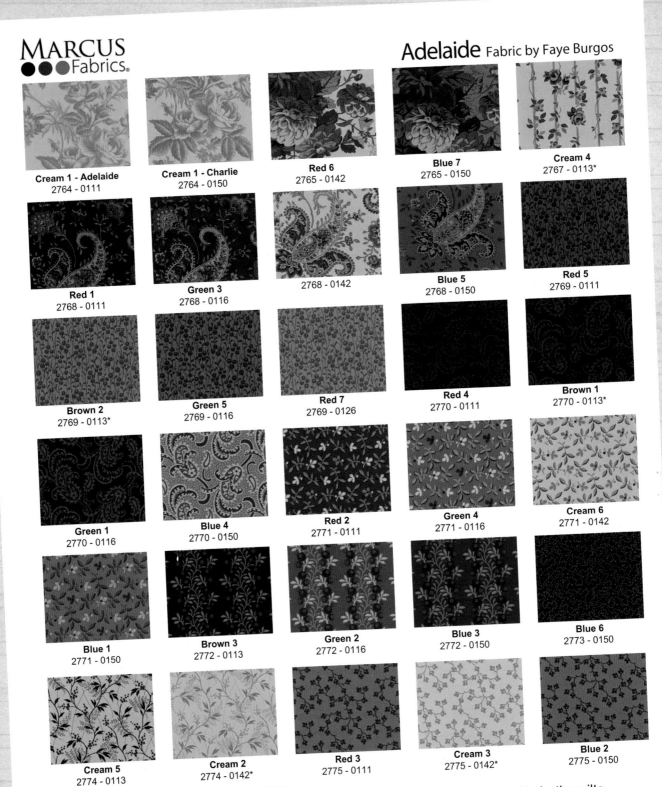

Cream 1 - Adelaide
2764 - 0111

Cream 1 - Charlie
2764 - 0150

Red 6
2765 - 0142

Blue 7
2765 - 0150

Cream 4
2767 - 0113*

Red 1
2768 - 0111

Green 3
2768 - 0116

2768 - 0142

Blue 5
2768 - 0150

Red 5
2769 - 0111

Brown 2
2769 - 0113*

Green 5
2769 - 0116

Red 7
2769 - 0126

Red 4
2770 - 0111

Brown 1
2770 - 0113*

Green 1
2770 - 0116

Blue 4
2770 - 0150

Red 2
2771 - 0111

Green 4
2771 - 0116

Cream 6
2771 - 0142

Blue 1
2771 - 0150

Brown 3
2772 - 0113

Green 2
2772 - 0116

Blue 3
2772 - 0150

Blue 6
2773 - 0150

Cream 5
2774 - 0113

Cream 2
2774 - 0142*

Red 3
2775 - 0111

Cream 3
2775 - 0142*

Blue 2
2775 - 0150

2776 - 0150

Aged Canvas
WR2 - Y139 - 0141

Patterns with an asterisk* are used in both quilts.

NOTE: Images on this page are for identification only.
Please refer to actual swatch card for accurate color & scale.

Notes:

*Look for Sarah and Dolores'
other Star Books.*

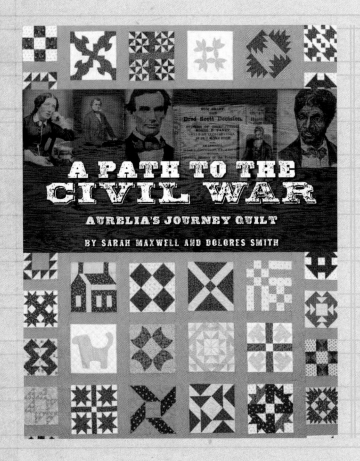

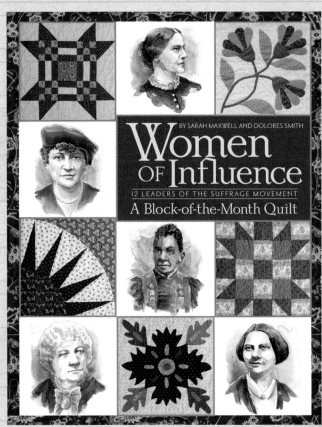

Sarah Maxwell and Dolores Smith of Homestead Hearth

Website: www.homesteadhearth.com

Blog: www.homesteadhearth.blogspot.com

Email: info@homesteadhearth.com

Bibliography:
Charles Tenney Civil War Letters, 1861-1863, Accession #11616, Albert H. Small Special Collections Library, University of Virginia, Charlottesville, Va.